Values in Education
in Northern Ireland

Alison Montgomery
Alan Smith

School of Education

University of Ulster

Acknowledgements

The authors are extremely grateful to the Northern Ireland Council for the Curriculum, Examinations and Assessment (CCEA) for providing the funds to undertake this study and for the professional support provided by Carmel Gallagher.

We would also like to express our sincere gratitude to the numerous teachers, educationists and others who gave so generously of their time during the course of the research.

Values in Education
in Northern Ireland

Alison Montgomery and Alan Smith

ISBN 1 85678 869 5

Contents

Chapter one

Introduction

The *Values in Education* project was commissioned by the Northern Ireland Council for the Curriculum, Examinations and Assessment (NICCEA) to be undertaken over a twelve month period between 1995 and 1996. The aims of the project were to:

- research existing approaches to values in education;
- generate specific 'profiles' of values initiatives in education; and
- evaluate the current provision for values in education in the Northern Ireland Curriculum.

This report documents the findings from the research undertaken into values in education within the Northern Ireland Curriculum and in the wider educational context of the UK and Europe. The report also presents some recommendations for further development in this area.

The original remit for the project included two further objectives relating to 'the development of a mechanism to help schools review current provision for values in education' and 'the development of guidance material on promoting values in education' for schools. For many teachers the project represented their first encounter with an explicit reference to values in the context of the curriculum and as a way of looking at their own subject area. It became clear that a significant amount of preparatory work would need to be undertaken within schools before any further instrument to help schools audit provision could be developed.

It also became apparent that the generation of guidance materials at this stage would be inappropriate. Such a move was perceived to be detrimental to securing teachers' support for and commitment to the advancement and dissemination of the values dimension. The reasons for this will hopefully become clear from the feedback from teachers presented later in this report. An over-riding factor however were persistent feelings amongst many teachers of overload, pressure and confusion as a result of "coming to terms with the new requirements of the Northern Ireland Curriculum".

Values and education - attempts at definition

The field of values and education has been the focus of study by educationalists and researchers for some considerable time. Much of this work has been located in Canada and the USA, though during the last decade a significant amount of literature has emerged in Europe (a selection of this literature is included in the bibliography to this report). An investigation of values and education covers a wide range of issues and this research uncovered a comprehensive and diverse list of topics and materials. In the international context, a European questionnaire survey concerning values and education revealed a considerable breadth and complexity to the many definitions of the term (Taylor 1993). Responses to the questionnaire from different countries located values within education using a number of descriptive terms. These included reference to moral, religious, cultural, aesthetic, democratic, national, personal, social and pastoral dimensions as part of whole school ethos as well as having implications for teaching and learning processes.

Within the UK researchers and educationists have identified similar perspectives and their relevance for curriculum subjects and cross-curricular themes. However, with the exception of Scotland, 'Values in Education' and 'Values Education' are not terms in common usage, but they are generally understood to refer to a comparatively broad, generic domain. This is reflected in the wide variety of research and development projects and publications which make explicit reference to values and values education or employ language synonymous with this area, while also focusing on content-related areas of the curriculum. The word 'values' is commonly considered a rather ambiguous term, and educational writers and researchers have therefore substituted other terms such as *attitudes, beliefs, ideals* and *principles.* Indeed these terms are often used interchangeably and this was corroborated by the language used by teachers and educationists in interviews. Individuals frequently expressed some discomfort using 'values' type words, and discussions often took place with perhaps little or no specific reference to these terms, although the subject matter was clearly value-laden. Similarly, some writers have been reluctant to categorise their work under a "values" heading (McPhail 1972; Taylor 1994), and others have identified possible advantages of using non-explicit 'values' type words.

Further discussion and debate has centred on the use of 'the preposition' in that some distinction has been made between 'Values Education' and 'Values *in* Education' (Barr 1995; Pickard 1995; SCCC 1991). Values Education is generally understood as distinct elements of school life or the curriculum, involving the examination and communication of an explicit set of values. Some educationists have expressed concern that values are perceived as a separate domain, as "another subject" to be included in the curriculum or simply as moral education. 'Values in Education' comprises a more comprehensive set of issues and activities, located throughout the whole school and wider education system. Every aspect of school life may be addressed through this definition; relationships, school ethos, discipline and behaviour. Most literature and curriculum materials generated in the values field tend not to dwell on the debate over the preposition, attending instead to the definition and perceptions of values within concrete educational settings. In order to avoid confusion with other values projects and activities, this report will refer to this project as *Values in Education (NI)*, and to the general values area as values and education.

It is worth noting the debate and confusion surrounding the distinction between values education and moral education. Writers have addressed this issue in different contexts (Berkowitz 1995; Haldane 1986; McLaughlin 1995; Wilson 1990). Moral education tends to focus upon principles of behaviour, relating to the distinction between right and wrong. Values education embraces morals along with principles, attitudes and ideals, but does not refer quite so directly to behaviour, and is not always associated with apparently unequivocal judgements of right and wrong (a common characteristic of moral education).

In specific terms, proponents of values education give it a broader definition than moral education, arguing that it incorporates an eclectic range of interests, as well as having religious and moral dimensions.

Perceptions of values and education

A review of current literature and interviews with teachers and others engaged in education, revealed a widespread acknowledgement that all educational activity is value-laden. Many individuals suggested that every comment, decision or action reflects or communicates some value or values, and that values permeate or "impregnate" the educational process (Bottery 1990:2; Taylor 1993:85; Tomlinson and Quinton 1986:7-8).

A number of bodies with statutory responsibility for education have demonstrated their agreement with the pervasive nature of values by referring to the role of values within the school in the production of policy documents.

The School Curriculum and Assessment Authority (SCAA) has produced several discussion papers on *Spiritual and Moral Development* and *Education for Adult Life: Spiritual Development of Young People*. SCAA suggests that schools draw up their own values statement outlining what values the school "intends to promote", and which values it "intends to demonstrate through all aspects of its life". The document describes values as "inherent in teaching", "at the heart of" and "underpinning" important aspects of school life such as expectations, rules and community (SCAA 1995). In October 1996 SCAA also launched a National Consultation on Values in Education and the Community. A series of values statements were issued on society, relationships, self and the environment, and responses were then sought from a wide range of statutory and voluntary bodies and individuals. This consultation is intended to inform the drafting of future guidance materials and school practice in spiritual, moral, social and cultural development (see Appendix 3).

The Scottish Consultative Council for the Curriculum (SCCC) has published a discussion document entitled *Values in Education* which outlines a "sense of the values which it seeks to promote" (SCCC 1991). The document was then offered to schools for discussion and action. The SCCC catalogue of educational publications and materials contains a section entitled Values, Climate and Ethos, again illustrating the Council's recognition of, and commitment to stimulating discussion and action in Values in Education.

In Northern Ireland, explicit reference is made to Values in Education by the Department of Education for Northern Ireland (DENI) in its strategic plan, which outlines the Department's priorities for education in the years leading up to the end of the century. One of the strategic aims referred to in the section entitled 'Learning for Life' is the "[nurturing] of moral values" and "respect for the worth of all individuals".

The *Values in Education (NI)* project has been undertaken as part of NICCEA's remit to help inform and guide policy and decision-making on matters related to the curriculum. The five year period from 1996 - 2001 has been earmarked as a period of planning and preparation to identify a vision for education in Northern Ireland for the new millennium. This stage of the project represents the beginning of a process to provide greater clarification of the values in and through the Northern Ireland Curriculum. It also provides the starting point for a further, developmental phase which investigates how values in education might be given more prominence within schools in a number of practical ways.

Outline of the report

The remainder of this report represents the outcomes from the first year of the *Values in Education (NI)* project.

Chapter 2 provides an outline of the methodology which was used to collate data and information as part of the fieldwork. The remaining chapters are organised in the following way.

Chapter 3 presents a review of initiatives in values and education within Europe, the UK, and Northern Ireland. Included in this review are details of organisations, bodies and individuals engaged in activities which are widely recognised as part of the values and education field (brief summaries of additional organisations and projects are also provided in Appendix 3).

Chapters 4, 5 and 6 represent a framework for understanding the research findings from this project. More than 60 teachers, principals, educationists and education advisers were interviewed about a range of topics related to education and values. Their responses are interpreted and presented under the headings for these three chapters:

- Values and the Formal Curriculum
- Values and the Informal Curriculum
- Values and the Hidden Curriculum.

Chapter 7 is a summary and presents some recommendations for the further development of Values in Education in Northern Ireland.

The Bibliography is an extensive list of publications related to the area of values and education. References include books, articles, journals, newsletters, curriculum materials and resources (including videos), guidance materials and discussion papers.

An index to the report is also provided.

Chapter two

Methodology

To fulfil the three main aims of the *Values in Education (NI)* project data was compiled using several research methods. An evaluation of the current provision for values in education in the Northern Ireland Curriculum formed a major part of the research, and in terms of fieldwork, constituted the greatest part. During the early planning stages of the project a decision was taken in consultation with CCEA not to undertake classroom observation or "tracking" exercises. The rationale for this was not to duplicate methods already underway as part of the NI Cohort Study (Harland et al 1996). Consideration was therefore given to other research approaches; surveys, questionnaires, formal and informal interviews. Surveys and questionnaires were regarded to be restrictive and imprecise considering the complex, sensitive, and often indeterminate nature of values. In addition, selecting pertinent and unambiguous questions was considered problematic, as was anticipating follow-up questions, without some prior knowledge of typical responses. The absence of immediacy in using questionnaires was also considered an obstacle, again because of the subject nature of the research.

For the reasons outlined above, interviews seemed to present the most effective means of collecting data. These were structured in a semi-formal manner, with an interview schedule designed prior to each interview, and provision made for departing from the schedule or extending the interview to address other issues, if they seemed appropriate and relevant.

Interviewees

A wide range of individuals involved in education in England, Scotland, the Republic of Ireland and Northern Ireland were contacted throughout the project and with the exception of a few, all contributed willingly to the project, by taking part in interviews and discussions, or by supplying information or materials.

The persons interviewed included the following:

- Advisors from five Education and Library Boards
- Assistant Advisors
- Field Officers
- Principals and Vice principals
- Class teachers
- EMU Co-ordinators
- Educational researchers
- Clergy
- Representatives from CCMS
- Officers from DENI and CCEA

- Staff from teacher training colleges
- Representatives from voluntary bodies and organisations
- Other interested individuals

Forty-two Board officers and twenty-four principals, vice-principals, class teachers and EMU co-ordinators were interviewed.

The Education and Library Board Officers were important informants for three reasons. Firstly, most had at least four years teaching experience (some had over twenty), and a thorough working knowledge and understanding of the Northern Ireland Curriculum (at least in their area of speciality), and of the issues and challenges currently facing teachers and pupils.

Secondly, many Board officers were seconded from their schools and had the opportunity to visit and interact with teachers in other schools, they had a degree of objectivity which they suggested other teachers may not have.

Thirdly, because of the nature of their advisory role Board officers have regular contact with many teachers in their subject area. In responding to the interview questions they often drew on these teachers' experiences as well as their own. They were therefore able to give many apposite and vivid examples in their responses.

In drawing up a list of Board officers and teachers for interview, attempts were made to include representatives for every subject and Key Stage of the Northern Ireland Curriculum (in order to comply with the remit for the project). Respondents therefore drew upon experiences and examples of:

all levels and types of schools

- Primary - Key Stage 1 and 2
  (Controlled, Maintained, Integrated)
- Post-Primary - Key Stage 3 and 4
  (Secondary, Grammar, Controlled, Maintained and Integrated)
- Special Schools

the Areas of Study in the Northern Ireland Curriculum

- Creative and Expressive
  (Art & Design, Drama, Media Studies, Music and Physical Education)
- English
- Environment and Society (Business Studies, Geography and History)
- Language Studies (French, German, Irish, and Spanish)
- Mathematics
- Personal and Social Education
- Science (Home Economics, Science and Technology)
- Religious Education

the Cross-Curricular Themes

- Careers Education
- Economic Awareness
- Education for Mutual Understanding (EMU)
- Cultural Heritage
- Health Education
- Information Technology.

In addition, respondents made references to, and provided examples of, issues and situations which were part of their experience beyond the classroom. Interviews also contained questions about individuals' roles and relationships in their schools and the wider education system.

The interview schedule

The interview questions raised a wide range of issues; curriculum subjects and materials, school policies and ethos, relationships and behaviour. In reviewing the current provision for values in the Northern Ireland Curriculum (essentially what is taught in the 4-16 Curriculum) the programmes of study and attainment targets for each subject at each of the four Key Stages, were analysed. An interview schedule was then devised containing a series of questions which focused on each Area of Study. Questions were of three main types:

Subject-specific questions which addressed:

- the range of possible definitions for the term "values";
- the awareness and identification of specific values and value-related topics in a specific subject;
- the 'perceived value' of a subject by teachers;
- the value messages communicated through a subject's attainment targets and assessment structures;
- the topics which presented difficulties for teachers;
- the issues and topics which could be addressed in developing guidance material on values in the curriculum;
- the role of EMU and other cross-curricular themes in a specific subject;
- opportunities available and/or taken to develop links with other subjects in value-related areas.

Context-specific questions which addressed:

- awareness and perception of values in special needs context;
- values in integrated schools;
- values and the Transfer Procedure;
- values in approaches to lower ability pupils;
- perceived differences in values between controlled, maintained, secondary, grammar, single sex, mixed, special and integrated schools.

Broader issues about teaching which addressed:

- values and EMU;
- approaches to and handling of controversial issues;
- priorities in the school timetable;
- the values embodied in classroom and school management;
- value aspects of various teaching strategies;
- perceptions of value dimension(s) in the curriculum;
- whole child development;
- gender issues;
- debates surrounding the changing role of teachers;
- the relationship between personal values and teacher identity.

Although questions were drafted to focus on Areas of Study rather than individual subjects, respondents tended to concentrate on their area of speciality in the curriculum. This might have been teaching History in the controlled secondary sector, or providing curriculum support for primary teachers in Science or English. The exceptions were Board Advisors who were responsible for three or four subjects within an Area of Study. They tended to respond to questions, by drawing on their knowledge and experience of all the subjects included within an Area of Study. An example of an interview schedule is provided in Appendix 1.

Arrangements for holding interviews were greatly influenced by Board officers' and teachers' timetables and workloads. The nature of each interview depended to a large extent on the respondent and time constraints. The duration of interviews therefore varied between 45 minutes and 1.5 hours. The opportunity to discuss additional areas was influenced by both the respondent and the time available.

Profiles of values initiatives

In order to compile listings of completed and ongoing initiatives in 'Values in Education' in the UK and Europe and to document present approaches to 'Values in Education' (a second aim of the project remit), a comprehensive selection of reports, projects and teaching materials was accessed and reviewed. Materials were sourced from various locations. In Northern Ireland, teachers and Board officers provided curriculum and guidance materials. Documents were also obtained from DENI and CCEA, and these dealt with a wide range of issues relevant to education and the wider society. The Schools Curriculum and Assessment Authority (SCAA), the Office for Standards in Education (OFSTED), the Scottish Consultative Council for the Curriculum (SCCC), HMI of schools in Scotland and the National Curriculum Council (NCC) also supplied a quantity of literature.

Publications, reports, classroom and school materials were also received from voluntary bodies and organisations and a variety of projects and programmes in Northern Ireland, Scotland and England.

In addition, participation at various conferences on 'Values in Education', 'Ethos and Performance Indicators' and 'School Evaluation' also supplemented the data collected through other methods. Such conferences gave participants the opportunity to gain information via interesting and informative presentations and to also acquire insights into the practicalities and realities of a range of research projects. These included 'Values Education in the Primary School', the development of values education materials, the formulation of school values policies, and implications of using 'Ethos Indicators' in school self-evaluation.

Chapter three

Profiles of values initiatives

The European context

Values in Education has become the focus of an international collaborative research venture initiated by the Consortium of Institutions for Development and Research in Education in Europe (CIDREE). This venture is known collectively as the *Values in European Education Project* (VEEP). In 1992 the VEEP was commissioned by UNESCO to undertake a project to contribute to its Humanistic and International Dimension of Education programme for 1990-1995. The project had three strands:-

• the provision of guidelines on values education for educational policy-makers, curriculum designers and teacher trainers (published as *A Sense of Belonging, Guidelines for Values for the Humanistic and International Dimension of Education,* UNESCO/CIDREE, 1994);

• the development and publication of an annotated bibliography (published as *Values Education in Europe: A Select Annotated Bibliography for 27 countries 1985-1992,* UNESCO/CIDREE, 1994);

• a questionnaire survey on values education in Europe and an overview of the annotated bibliographies of European countries (published as *Values Education in Europe: a comparative overview of a survey of 26 countries in 1993,* UNESCO/CIDREE, 1994) and (Taylor 1994:6-7).

The questionnaire survey produced a comprehensive summary of information on a range of issues associated with values education, including definitions and background, aims and objectives, formal curriculum provision, whole school and extra-curricular contributions, teacher training and teaching methods.

Eleven institutions in seven member countries (including NICCEA) are participating in the VEEP collaborative programme, which is described as a "framework for sharing and discussing aspects of values education" (UNESCO ed. Barr, 1994:2).

13

The project adopts a curricular approach and focuses on a "range of strategies, guidelines and experimental approaches in the field of values education" ibid:6). To give greater definition to such guidelines, the range of approaches adopted in values education projects in several European countries was illustrated. These addressed areas such as values and consensus, citizenship, democracy and education, and values in national and world communities.

The intention was to identify common elements in these projects and to clarify what were perceived as "essentially straightforward ideas" to "underpin the clarification and communication of values for the enhancement of the humanistic and international dimension of education" (ibid:9). This culminated in a series of recommendations for schools, accompanied by practical suggestions as to how schools might promote the objectives embraced in the recommendations (see Appendix 2).

The VEEP is intended to contribute substantially to the wider UNESCO programme. At the meeting of the Secretaries General of European National Commissions for UNESCO in 1990, recognition was given to the importance of the theme 'Education, culture, human rights and international understanding'. A synthesis and discussion paper was prepared and this was followed in 1991 by an international workshop and the launch of the programme. The VEEP helps locate the *Values in Education (NI)* project within the wider context of European education.

The European Values Study 1981-1990.

The European Values Study 1981-1990 was undertaken by the European Values Group (EVG) - an informal network of social scientists, philosophers, theologians and researchers, drawn from universities and commercial agencies committed to values research. This study addressed a variety of European value issues, including the debate over common values, changing values, the permeation of Christian values through society, the potential replacement of a Christian values system, and the implications of European unity. An analysis of the responses then suggested some possible ramifications for education. Firstly, attention was focused on the potential influence of other "over-riding forces" which are "value-laden", and which could exert a greater influence than values developed within individual educational institutions. Secondly, those engaged in education were informed of their responsibility "to understand values in society" and their ability to "influence values in education". Thirdly, in discerning the future of education, significance was attributed to values linked with issues such as "enterprise", and to the processes of education "which lead to greater autonomy" and which provide the individual with "a greater sense of responsibility for [his/her] own future" (McGettrick, European Values Group: 1992:52-56).

The Curriculum Redefined project

The Curriculum Redefined project was developed by the Organisation for Economic Co-operation and Development (OECD) and the Centre for Educational Research and Innovation (CERI). This incorporates a programme on Humanities and Values Education (Moon 1993, *Humanities and Arts Education*: A Review of Issues prepared as part of the OECD/CERI Project, The Curriculum Redefined).

The Commonwealth Values in Education project

A working paper entitled *Commonwealth Values in Education* was prepared for the Commonwealth Secretariat in 1994 as part of an initiative based at the University of London (Bourne 1994). The paper is based on responses received to a Citizenship and Human Rights questionnaire circulated to educational authorities throughout Commonwealth countries. Recommendations accompanying the paper suggested the creation of a database for the exchange of materials and the recruitment of teachers and examination and curriculum bodies to "provide necessary in-school support...and give further consideration to material needs and more general questions of school effectiveness". Following the publication of this paper, a preliminary meeting was held by representatives from a number of countries, and it was decided that each country would undertake its own research into pupils' perceptions and definitions of the term 'human rights' with the intention of bringing these findings together to identify strategies for further development.

Statutory approaches to values and education in the UK

Within the UK a substantial body of values and education literature has been produced and a considerable number of statutory and voluntary research projects have been completed or are at various stages of completion. A directory compiled by Taylor (1994), records the range and extent of academic work and activities in the area of values and education for the period 1988-1993. It includes brief details of 113 projects and a selected bibliography of over 200 publications. Associations, organisations and centres undertaking values research and/or activities are also listed. Profiles of a selection of these and other research and development activities will be presented below (a more comprehensive bibliography of organisations and projects is included in Appendix 3).

The emergence of an increasingly diverse and pluralistic society in England and Wales and the implications of educational reform have instigated questions and concern about the moral and social development of children and young people, and the nature of their role as active citizens in the local, national and international community. Attention has focused on the formal curriculum, that is the National Curriculum with reference to evidence the provision made for the individual pupil's personal growth and development.

The National Curriculum Council (NCC)

The National Curriculum Council's guidance on *The Whole Curriculum* clearly sets out what it perceives as the "duty" of the education system. This is defined as,

> to encourage pupils to think and act for themselves, with an *acceptable set of personal qualities and values* which also meet the wider social demands of adult life. (NCC 1990:7, author's italics).

In its discussion document on *Spiritual and Moral Development* emphasis is placed on the importance of the school-home partnership towards,

> furnishing pupils with the knowledge and the ability to question and reason which will *enable them to develop their own value system* and to make responsible decisions on such matters. (NCC 1993:5).

The School Curriculum and Assessment Authority (SCAA)

In a revision of this paper by the School Curriculum and Assessment Authority in 1995, schools are encouraged to identify and document a statement of values which will permeate school life and to which staff, pupils and parents will agree and identify with. It was emphasised that such a statement should not be a glossy brochure, but rather "an essential and honest statement about the school and what it stands for" and one which would be "implemented - that it not only be seen, but be seen to be effective" (SCCA 1995:9).

The Dearing Report

In a final report on the National Curriculum (*The National Curriculum and its Assessment*, 1994) to the Secretary of State for Education, reference was made to the educational challenge underpinning the National Curriculum. It was stated that,

> Education is not concerned only with equipping students with the knowledge and skills they need to earn a living. (Its intention is also to encourage students) to respect others, to become good citizens, to think things out for themselves, to use their time creatively and pursue a healthy lifestyle and not least, value themselves and their achievements.
>
> (Dearing 1994)

The main thrust of values education in the National Curriculum is, to a large extent, represented through the cross-curricular themes and perhaps most vividly through Education for Citizenship.

Education for Citizenship

In a speech given by the Secretary of State for Education in 1990, schools were encouraged to lay the foundations for positive, participative citizenship by helping pupils' to acquire and understand essential information, and by providing them with opportunities and incentives to participate in all aspects of school life (*Curriculum Guidance No.8*).

The objectives of Education for Citizenship include:

• the development and understanding of knowledge about community and society;
• the promotion and advancement of cross-curricular skills in communication, numeracy and study;
• the promotion and development of positive attitudes concerning individual duties, responsibilities and rights as well as respect for democracy;
• the development of pupils' personal moral codes and the exploration of values and beliefs. Pupils are encouraged to identify shared values, to explore and consider solutions to moral dilemmas, to discuss differences and resolve conflict, and to appreciate how certain factors such as time and experience may influence personal values and beliefs.

The guidance materials suggest eight inter-related content areas which should be explored in and through curriculum provision. These are:

- the nature of community;
- roles and relationships in a pluralist society;
- duties, rights and responsibilities of being a citizen;
- the family;
- democracy in action;
- the citizen and law;
- work, employment and leisure;
- public services.

Suggestions are also given for establishing a whole-school policy based on the aims of Education for Citizenship as well as opportunities for where the theme may be incorporated in the formal curriculum.

The Office for Standards in Education (OFSTED)

The Office for Standards in Education (OFSTED) published a discussion paper in 1994 focusing on the types of values encouraged and communicated through the curriculum and personal relationships in schools. The paper contextualises values within the framework of "spiritual, moral, social and cultural development" (SMSC) which is one of the four statutory elements outlined for inspection in OFSTED's *Framework for Inspection* 1993 (revised).

The main objective of the paper is to encourage debate on the values and principles underlying SMSC in order to work towards greater national consensus regarding provision and to identify possible criteria for use in inspection. Schools are reminded of their obligation to promote SMSC development and the intention to evaluate this development as part of the inspection process. In approaching evaluation it is suggested that firm standards may be set for personal behaviour based on,

pupils' knowledge, skills and understanding;

appropriate and high standards of behaviour; and

a fully developed view of the nature and quality of the educational processes [underpinning] pupils' development.

(OFSTED 1994)

The Scottish Consultative Council for the Curriculum (SCCC)

In Scotland, the Scottish Consultative Council for the Curriculum (SCCC) has stated its commitment to supporting and maintaining resources for the ongoing development of values in education. In pursuing this goal, the Council has produced a number of publications on values in education, including a series entitled *Perspectives* which examines issues relating to school climate and ethos. Other materials have included:

• *Values in Education*, (1991) which contained a statement outlining the "sense of values which the Council seeks to promote";

• *The Heart of the Matter*, (1995) which discusses the importance of personal and social education; and

• *Sharing Responsibility* (1995) which investigates opportunities for schools in Europe to share responsibility and understand the influences affecting young people's lives.

SCCC has considered values in the context of the whole curriculum and value-related issues have been addressed in many publications, including for example, *PSE 5-14 exemplification: The Whole School Approach - A Staff Development Workshop,* (1995). This contains materials and guidance for workshops, which deal with attitudes, relationships and skills,

> likely to aid the promotion and development of a positive and supportive school atmosphere in which the personal and social development of all pupils may be fostered. (SCCC 1995)

The SCCC has also produced, *Working Together: A Pack for Parents and Teachers*, (1993) and *A Sense of Belonging* (Reflections on Curricular Issues, 1995).

Schools Inspectorate in Scotland

Over the last five years, HM Inspectorate in Scottish Schools has developed a major school evaluation scheme based on a set of educational indicators to encourage and promote school development. These indicators are a mechanism with which schools may evaluate their effectiveness and quality, focusing on two main areas - performance and ethos. In 1992, HMI published two documents relating to performance in primary and post-primary schools (HMI:1992) and these also contained a number of indicators relating to school ethos. There are twelve indicators in all, covering a range of issues - staff and pupil morale, discipline, relationships, school management, the pastoral dimension and the physical environment. The 'Ethos Indicators' programme was designed to enable staff, pupils and parents to assess and evaluate the teaching and learning experiences in their school. Through the use of different research methods (interviews, questionnaires and surveys) responses are recorded to a range of issues which have been selected by the head teacher or senior management team for consideration.

A phrase synonymous with 'Ethos and Performance Indicators' is 'collective self-evaluation' which aspires to provide everyone who is part of the school community an opportunity to comment on the effectiveness and quality of the school. Schools in many regions of Scotland have become involved in this evaluation scheme and similar sets of indicators are being developed in England and Northern Ireland. The feedback from participating schools has been very favourable with teachers commenting that the findings from the indicators process enabled school boards to use their powers in a constructive and supportive way; that relationships had been improved; and that the acknowledgement of a wider range of views led to schools having greater credibility with teachers, parents, and the wider community.

Non-statutory initiatives on values and education within the UK

In England, there are a number of organisations and centres engaged in research and development activities widely recognised as being within the field of values and education. These projects address issues such as ethos, citizenship, pastoral care and moral and social development as well as specific aspects of values education.

The Citizenship Foundation

The Citizenship Foundation seeks to "improve and extend the quality of citizenship, particularly through education". The Foundation has produced various citizenship materials on human rights, consumerism, ethics and political education for primary and post-primary schools and adult education groups. It also undertakes research, organises school competitions and publishes a bi-annual journal entitled *Citizenship* .

A recent publication has been *You, Me, Us! Social and Moral Responsibility for primary schools* (eds. Rowe and Newton:1994). This pack was produced as a result of co-operation between the Citizenship Foundation and The Home Office. Following a discussion of the theoretical background and teaching methods, five citizenship issues (friendship, rules, property and power, respecting differences and community and the environment), are explored through a variety of activities.

The Values Education Council

In October 1995, the Values Education Council held its first annual conference and AGM in London. The Council has been established by individuals engaged in activities in the field of values and education to

> promote and develop values education and values in education, and to help individuals develop as responsible and caring persons and live as participating members of a pluralist society.
> (Constitution of The Values Education Council).

The Council's aims include the promotion of dialogue and research into values, the development of a network for exchanging and discussing information and the provision of a framework for member bodies and developers of public policy to work together.

NAVET

The National Association for Values in Education and Training (NAVET) identifies its main objectives as developing an understanding and communication of values and their application within education and training, and encouraging a recognition of the diversity of values and opinions in society and of the powerful influence values systems may have upon the climate of organisations. NAVET also produces a regular newsletter and a short papers series.

RIMSCUE

The Centre for Research into Moral, Spiritual and Cultural Understanding and Education (RIMSCUE Centre) is based at the University of Plymouth. It is primarily a research body, examining such issues as the moral, spiritual and cultural development of children, ethos, the hidden curriculum and values in education.

The Gordon Cook Foundation

The Gordon Cook Foundation, based in Aberdeen is a charitable organisation which seeks to promote and advance "all aspects of education which are likely to [further] character development and citizenship". A major aspect of the Foundation's work has been to fund and support research and development projects and activities which further its objectives of investing in people and "effective organisations" and which promote the development of teachers and values education within the educational system.

Over the past five years, the Foundation has funded over 100 projects exploring a variety of issues, including the preparation and trialling of values education materials for teacher training and classroom use, investigations into parental values, the transmission of values in the pre-school environment, and the identification and communication of values in primary and post-primary schools. (Further details of projects funded by the Gordon Cook Foundation may be found in Appendix 3). Many of the organisations and projects mentioned in this chapter have also received funding support from the Foundation.

VECTOR

Values Education, Consultancy, Training and Organisational Research (VECTOR Fellowship) is part of an independent research and training consultancy. It provides information on values education, identifies and disseminates good practice, pursues training and organisational development opportunities and supports a network of interested bodies through a regular newsletter.

Projects and publications

In addition to the projects and activities undertaken by the organisations listed above there are many others which have been initiated by individuals educational bodies or universities (details of these are included in Appendix 3).

Values and Visions

The 'Values and Visions' project, part of the Manchester Development Education Project is a national project established "to encourage spiritual development and global awareness in the primary school". The aim is to reach teachers "where they are" and to examine ways in which a school could evolve a "shared understanding of its own values and vision" by engaging in practical activities designed for whole school participation. In practical terms, the project offers in-service courses for teachers and school-based training to management, staff, parents, and pupils. Several 'Values and Visions' workshops have been held in Northern Ireland, offering teachers an opportunity to take "time out" and reflect upon their perceptions and experiences of teaching and to participate in discussion sessions on school values and visions.

The Nuffield Foundation

The Nuffield Foundation has recently published a National Curriculum design and technology course for Key Stage 3 (Nuffield Design and Technology Study Guide/Student's Book 1995). This has been devised in such a way as to allow explicit consideration of the position and relevance of values in design and technology. The project approaches values in three ways.

Firstly, through an appraisal of real life case studies, pupils are encouraged to discuss the range of possible effects and implications of certain designs and technology and in turn, pertinent value-related issues.

Secondly, with the provision of a values template, pupils are prompted to analyse what values are implicit in the design and construction tasks which they undertake. The template is essentially comprised of sets of values (technological, environmental, economic, aesthetic, social and moral) which pupils are encouraged to consider when preparing their designs and constructions.

The third strand presents strategies for engaging with value issues. 'Winners and Losers' examines the positive and negative impact of designs and technology, identifying who will be directly or indirectly affected by specific technology, how they will be affected, and the appropriateness of the technology. A scoring system is used as part of the 'Winners and Losers' strategy, along with a pre-defined set of criteria.

Teachers are furnished with guidance and resources throughout the course, enabling them to promote pupils' development and understanding, and to deal more effectively and confidently with the values dimension of design and technology.

The Values Education Project

The 'Values Education Project' at Northern College, Dundee was undertaken over a five year period and considered a number of value areas including the theoretical, practical and applied nature of moral living; pluralistic Scottish society and Christian tradition; the schools' role as a community and its relationship with the wider community; individual and social dimensions of moral living; and specific and local concerns and global responsibilities. In practical terms, the project involved work with schools, a series of workshops and the production of guidance material entitled, *Values Education Project - A handbook for School Values Development.* This manual is divided into various sections and examines the experiences and approaches to values development in schools; the development and implementation of a statement of position on values; ethos and staff development; the audit and management of change in schools.

Academic publications

The philosophical nature of values has been explored by different researchers with studies examining the fundamental importance of values in determining how an individual ought to live his or her life (Almond 1981,1990; Carr 1991, 1992, 1993; Haldane 1986, 1990, 1993, 1994; Wilson 1977, 1979, 1986, 1987). Morality and ethics and their relationship with values have been common areas for discussion. Writers have explored definitions of morals and values, the perceived overlap of the two and the role of values and morals in religious education. In general, morals are perceived to be principles of behaviour relating especially to distinctions of right and wrong, while values are seen to embrace morals along with principles, attitudes, ideals and beliefs, and are not always associated with unequivocal judgements of right and wrong.

A recently published resource of practical relevance to schools is Cross (1995),*Values Education: A Staff Development Manual for Secondary Schools.* In this publication, guidance is offered to teachers to assist them to fulfil government requirements outlined by OFSTED for values education in schools, by addressing the 'what' and 'how' of values education. The pack contains theoretical material and practical examples of classroom activities; a consideration of the nature and purpose of values; curriculum concerns; and values education and the whole school. The aim is to help teachers "create... effective lessons" and "tackle values education with confidence."

Journals and newsletters

There are a number of journals and newsletters in circulation which are concerned with different aspects of values and education. The *Journal of Moral Education* is described as a "unique interdisciplinary, international forum for moral education and development", and publishes papers on all aspects of the theory and practice of moral education.

NAVET (see p. 21) publishes the *NAVET Papers*, a series of short papers on any aspect of values within education and training and *Newsvalues* - a bi-annual newsletter. VECTOR (see p. 22) produces *VECTOR NEWS*.

Values Education published by St. Martin's College, Lancaster aims to provide a forum for discussion of issues in values education, inviting contributions on any aspect of social and moral education, personal values and human relations.

Courses

Activities include the provision of long-term and short-term courses which address the general concept of values and education.

A modular Masters degree is offered in Values Education at the Institute of Education in London, giving teachers the opportunity to reflect in a philosophical and systematic way on the values underlying their practice.

A Masters degree may be taken in Religious Education-Moral Education at St. Martin's College, Lancaster. This course aims "to deepen teachers' understanding of religion and ethics and their interfaces as relevant to their professional contexts" (Taylor 1994). A B.Ed Honours degree in Moral Education/Social Ethics and a PGCE in RE-ME are also offered.

Other courses provide short-term exposure to specific values issues in teaching practice and the curriculum. Such courses include Values Education and Spiritual Development in the Primary School, and Personal and Social Development of Children through Primary Education (St. Martin's College, Lancaster).

The Centre for Religious Education Development and Research (CREDAR) and RIMSCUE (see p. 21) also focus on values in teacher training courses.

Initiatives in values and education in Northern Ireland

While 'values' and 'values in education' are not terms in common usage within the Northern Ireland educational system, there does seem to be a prevailing awareness among teachers and educationists of the range of concepts and issues involved. The majority of value initiatives identified in Northern Ireland therefore do not make explicit reference to values or to the promotion or development of values. The aims and objectives of organisations included in this section and the nature of their activities does however indicate a strong commitment to the broader generic area of personal and community development, of which values and values education are an integral part.

The Department of Education for Northern Ireland (DENI)

In its recent consultative document, *A Strategic Analysis* , the Department of Education for Northern Ireland (DENI) makes reference to the government's priorities for education. It suggests that education has a major role to play in "developing appropriate values and attitudes in school life, such as personal integrity and consideration for others" (DENI 1995, p.3:2.3). Values are mentioned explicitly in a strategic plan formulated by DENI and published by DENI. Under the heading of Personal Development, a set of strategic aims are listed with reference to values. These are to nurture:

- moral values and a sense of personal responsibility;
- respect for diversity and for the worth of all individuals; and
- concern for other people, and appreciation of the value of co-operation and team effort.

(DENI 1995)

There is also a call for a commitment to promoting "a peaceful and tolerant society and appreciation of our natural and cultural inheritance". These aims along with the other aims and principles are perceived as providing definition to the nature of the Education Service and of contributing towards a clearer view of the direction of education for the immediate and long-term future.

In *A Strategic Analysis* reference is also made to the importance of "promoting mutual understanding between the two traditions within Northern Ireland, especially within the context of school life" (DENI 1995, p.3:2.3). A practical initiative introduced in pursuit of this objective is the 'Cross Community

Contact Scheme'. Approximately one-third of all schools in Northern Ireland are involved in this scheme which provides modest grants for collaborative projects between two or more schools which fulfil specific criteria (relating to the age and denomination of the pupils involved and the nature of the project). In addition, DENI has also supported smaller scale European projects which have sought to bring young people into contact with their contemporaries in other countries as well as increasing their knowledge and understanding of European and world affairs through curriculum subjects.

The Northern Ireland Curriculum

The structure and content of the Northern Ireland Curriculum was devised with the intent that it would be "broad, balanced and relevant" and that it would "meet the needs of pupils". With these objectives in mind, the Northern Ireland Curriculum has been defined in terms of areas of study (rather than subjects) with the intention of promoting a sense of "wholeness" in pupils' learning experience. In contrast with the National and Scottish Curricula, the Northern Ireland Curriculum has six *statutory* themes which schools are obliged to implement. These include Education for Mutual Understanding (EMU) and Cultural Heritage which have been identified as a perceptible values dimension within the curriculum. An increasing emphasis on the development of whole school policies (in particular pastoral care and discipline) has also turned teachers' attention to "value areas" (Hamill 1995).

In providing guidance towards the interpretation and implementation of the Northern Ireland Curriculum, a number of aims were outlined for advancement through the areas of study and statutory cross-curricular themes. These focused on the spiritual, moral, cultural, intellectual and physical development of pupils. A review of these various aims in the curriculum, and an analysis of how they might be advanced through individual subjects was undertaken by the Northern Ireland Council for the Curriculum, Examinations and Assessment (NICCEA). The study revealed that the curriculum yielded many opportunities for the promotion of these aims as well as providing evidence of recurrent themes and the overlap of certain issues and topics between the subjects.

A review of the revised curriculum revealed a preoccupation on the part of teachers with the intricate detail of statutory elements and in particular with the requirements associated with individual subjects. This concern with the subjects was perceived to be detrimental to the degree of attention given by teachers to cross-curricular themes and various steps have been instigated to encourage greater integration of these through the delivery of the curriculum. Strategies include clarifying the contribution of each subject to the themes; providing examples in curriculum guidance materials of how and where subjects meet objectives of the themes; and indicating the relevance of the themes at each of the key stages. To allow teachers time and space for further contemplation of the themes and aims, and consideration of how they might address them in their teaching situation, a five year moratorium on change has been imposed until the year 2001. The 'Values in Education' project was initiated at the beginning of this period, with one of its objectives being to evaluate the current provision for values in the curriculum and to inform the Council in its realisation of a vision for education in Northern Ireland for the next millennium.

Education for Mutual Understanding (EMU)

As already indicated, EMU has been identified as a strong values dimension in the curriculum. One of six (educational) cross-curricular themes, EMU became statutory under the 1989 Education Reform Order (NI) although many schools were engaged in EMU activities before the theme was formally included in the NI curriculum.

There are numerous statutory and non-statutory bodies presently undertaking activities related to EMU and its complementary theme Cultural Heritage. A selection of these organisations and their work is presented in this chapter. A list of organisations along with a brief description of their activities is included in Appendix 3.

EMU is involved with an explicit set of values through both the formal and informal curriculum. EMU aims to provide pupils with opportunities,

> to learn to respect and value themselves and others;
> to appreciate the interdependence of people within society;
> to know about and understand what is shared as well as what is different about their cultural traditions;
> to appreciate how conflict may be handled in non-violent ways.
>
> (NICC 1990)

In-service training for EMU is provided by the five local authorities (Education and Library Boards). Taught modules in EMU are also offered on postgraduate diploma courses at Queen's University, Belfast and the University of Ulster.

These courses employ interactive teaching methods to explore a range of issues relating to EMU including background, rationale, research, implementation, pedagogy and the teaching of controversial issues.

The Council for Catholic Maintained Schools (CCMS) has acknowledged its commitment to EMU and its role in fostering improved relationships. It has described EMU as the fourth 'R' (relationships), suggesting it should become a central element in the educational process. CCMS has issued statements on the development of EMU as part of its involvement in programmes known as Whole School Initiatives, Curriculum and Community; and Boards of Governors have been encouraged to demonstrate their commitment to EMU by supporting school initiatives and activities in this area.

The Forum on Community Understanding and Schools (FOCUS) is an informal network of individuals and organisations committed to forwarding the aims of EMU and Cultural Heritage through a variety of activities and support for teachers. Originally formed as a mutual support group for seconded teachers, it now comprises over thirty statutory and voluntary bodies. Many of these are pursuing value-related activities in schools and the wider community. A list of these organisations is provided in Appendix 3.

'The EMU Promoting School' is an action-based research project developed from the work of the 'Quaker Peace Education Project'. The emphasis of the project is on the "design, development and delivery" of long-term whole-school programmes centring around issues such as "self-esteem, the quality of relationships, conflict resolution skills, peer mediation training and bullying" (*Who's Who in EMU*, 1995:21). The main thrust of the project to date has been to establish partnerships with a small number of schools, focusing quite deliberately on the development of a positive ethos and involving teachers, pupils and the local community.

The 'Peer Mediation' programme is a further element of the 'EMU Promoting School Project' and is currently being developed in several schools in the Western and North Eastern Education and Library Boards. A long-term aim is to promote peer mediation in schools throughout Northern Ireland. The main aims of the programme are to promote children's understanding and management of conflict and to encourage and empower them to deal with their own arguments and disagreements. Training workshops are provided for children in Primary 7 with a view to them serving as mediators for the children in their schools.

The 'Speak Your Piece' Project is a research and development project funded by the European Commission and based within the School of Education at the University of Ulster. It has been set up in partnership with Channel 4 Schools, Ulster Television and the Youth Council for Northern Ireland. The project is concerned with the teaching of controversial issues. A series of five television programmes have been produced around the themes of identity, culture, religion and politics and support materials have been developed. The programmes have been used with 14-17 year olds in schools and youth organisations throughout Northern Ireland as the basis for discussion and debate on controversial issues.

Whole School Approaches

Increasing attention has been given to issues which affect the whole school, that is staff, pupils, parents and in some cases the wider community. Two of the Education and Library Boards have appointed advisors to deal exclusively with whole-school issues. Other Boards have included whole-school issues (WSI) as part of the remit of named advisors. Included under the umbrella of WSI is the preparation and implementation of pastoral care and discipline policies. In-service courses have been offered to teachers (often senior management), providing guidance and support towards identifying suitable and applicable strategies and mechanisms for school development. The Regional Training Unit (RTU) has also held workshops and courses on pastoral care provision for teachers and senior managers, giving practical guidance and support in framing and implementing a whole-school policy.

The Council for Catholic Maintained Schools (CCMS) has produced a series of guidelines on whole-school curriculum policy and school development planning. In outlining a "basic philosophy" for Catholic whole school policy, emphasis is laid on the school's whole community responsibility "to recognise its values, gifts and riches". It is also states that "an effective school policy is one in which values and attitudes concerning relationships between individuals and groups are lived out and not merely advocated" (CCMS 1991). In a second paper entitled *From Policy to Planning for Development,* Catholic schools are reminded of the importance of viewing the curriculum as the "totality of experiences which a school has to offer" and the centrality of the child in this educational process.

In 1995, the Department of Education in Northern Ireland (DENI) introduced the 'Raising School Standards Initiative'. This was developed in response to concerns surrounding under-achievement in some schools, and in particular, low levels of literacy and numeracy. *A Strategic Analysis* indicated a need to "target these schools in resource terms and to address other ways of helping underachieving schools to improve pupils performance" (DENI 1994, p.17,4.33).

Within the Western Education and Library Board, the 'Raising School Standards Initiative' was introduced in September 1995 under the title, 'The Developing School' project. Following inspection, approximately twenty primary and post-primary schools in the WELB were identified by DENI and invited to participate in the project. A liaison officer (who is also a subject advisor with the Board) has been appointed to provide guidance and support for each of the schools involved. The intention in the initial stages is that staff within each school will formulate an action plan, so that they can determine which issues need most attention and what progress they hope to achieve. The initiative encourages the involvement of parents, governors and the wider school community at appropriate stages.

Schools have developed individual programmes which concentrate on the formal curriculum and improving levels of literacy. Some schools have also focused on issues such as the school community; the pupil's experience of the transition from primary to secondary; pastoral care; and the general learning environment of the school. Once an action plan has been forwarded to the WELB, it is considered by the management group for 'The Developing Schools Initiative' and if approved funding is allocated.

Another project under development is 'The Strabane Initiative'. This project is "targeting all phases of educational provision from pre-school to Further Education". It aims to involve teachers, parents, and children as well as voluntary and statutory agencies in the local Strabane community, in addressing "the incidence of under-performance, by the funding of an imaginative range of measures in response to locally identified need." (WELB 1995)

A list of objectives have been identified, including an improvement in "the quality of parenting, achieving a closer match between the aims and aspirations of the schools and parents" and "raising the self-esteem and educational aspirations of children and young people within the community". The project is financed by the WELB for a three year period from 1995 and a number of proposals within the scheme are at various stages of conception and development.

A European dimension

The concept of European awareness and the implications of European Community policies for education and training were the focus of a research and development project commissioned by the Northern Ireland Curriculum Council (now NICCEA) in 1992. The project outcomes were disseminated through a set of guidance materials entitled *Thinking European - Ideas for Integrating a European Dimension into the Curriculum.* As well as giving examples of how and where the European dimension might be introduced through the four key stages, various possible aims and objectives were outlined towards the development of pupils' knowledge and understanding of European issues. These included an appreciation and awareness of the variety and differences between European cultures; cultivating tolerant and accepting attitudes towards other peoples' opinions, beliefs and ideas; and developing pupils' sense of responsibility as citizens of Europe, with particular attention being given to human rights, democracy, peace and the environment. In order to assist schools define and promote these values and attitudes in a progressive and coherent manner, strategies for managing a whole school approach were also presented.

Summary

This chapter has provided a broad overview of the projects and activities completed or in progress in the values and education field in Europe and the UK. It documents examples of the types of approaches being taken and indicates the different aspects of the curriculum which have been considered. It also outlines the extent to which statutory, academic and voluntary initiatives concerning values and education have been developed by organisations in Northern Ireland, although in most cases these have not involved an explicit approach to highlight the values underlying different initiatives.

Chapter four

Values and the formal curriculum

Prior to the commencement of this project there has not been a formal study of 'Values in Education' in Northern Ireland. A review of current educational projects and programmes does suggest however, that there are many activities and approaches which are in essence, value-oriented. These include activities of the kind referred to in the previous chapter, as well as others located in the different dimensions of school life, for example through whole-school issues, pastoral policy statements and individual school practice. Further examples will be explored in this chapter.

The statutory basis for the Northern Ireland Curriculum places an explicit emphasis on physical, moral, spiritual and cultural development - areas which are widely recognised as dominant characteristics of values education. There is however no obligation on schools to timetable any kind of values or moral education or to explore the conceptual dimensions of morals or values. The quality of teaching and learning in the values domain remains largely dependent on the teacher and school in question. A preliminary survey of the curriculum locates the values-related dimensions in ethos or climate; the notion of whole child development; welfare systems; some extra-curricular activities; and curriculum areas such as Religious Education (RE), Health Education (HE), Personal and Social Education (PSE) and aspects of cross curricular themes such as Education for Mutual Understanding (EMU).

Reference has already been made to the inclusion of values statements in statutory guidance and policies. DENI and CCEA both acknowledge the importance and significance of a values dimension in pupils' learning experiences and personal development. Indeed DENI has recently identified values and personal development as a key priority in teachers' presentation and pupils' comprehension of the Northern Ireland Curriculum (DENI 1995).

Initial reactions to the research

Because of the pervasive nature of values, very many aspects of the curriculum and school life were touched upon throughout the research. Discussions with respondents alone uncovered many issues, culminating in a plethora of data. Responses from the majority of individuals intimated a natural interest and concern in this whole area and many welcomed the opportunity to discuss values and related issues, as the opportunity had not previously presented itself.

Initial reactions from respondents were varied. Some teachers were rather confused as they attempted to locate values in the context of their experiences of teaching and the curriculum. Others were quite uncomfortable with the use of values-type language, expressing concern over its potential impact on curriculum interpretation and issues of teacher accountability. There was a tangible reluctance by a small number to even consider that they might bear any responsibility for the interpretation or communication of values through their teaching. While they agreed that values were inherent in education, they expressed feelings of discomfort, confusion and self-doubt, in dealing with values-related issues in any explicit sense. The majority of respondents took a little time to contemplate the concept of values in education and to *"adjust their way of thinking about the curriculum"* before reflecting on their perceptions and experiences in this area.

Teachers suggested the term was rather nebulous and difficult to *"pin down"* in the context of the curriculum. The whole area of values was described as *"immense"* and *"complex"* and individuals expressed some difficulty supplying a suitable definition. A few observed that there was an inadequate pool of vocabulary on which to draw when they came to articulating views and opinions. As indicated in the Introduction, respondents did substitute other terms, using them interchangeably throughout discussions, so reflecting the perceived ambiguity of the area. Despite these difficulties, there was widespread agreement that values permeated teaching and learning experiences and that it was not possible to divorce values from daily activities occurring within the education system.

Identifying a structure

In order to provide a more focused context in which to discuss values in education, and to identify a structure which would indicate the implications of values in education in more concrete terms, values were considered within three frameworks.

These were defined as follows:

1. The Curricular Framework

   includes the Formal, Informal and Hidden curricula. This provided a broad and accessible framework in which to review the current provision for and perceptions of values in education. The three curricula represent three major areas of school life, though there is some variation in the definition and application of the three curricular terms:

   - the *Formal Curriculum* is essentially the 'taught' curriculum. It encompasses the Areas of Study (and individual subjects), represented in the Northern Ireland Curriculum. In this report it pertains to the delivery and interpretation of subjects and cross-curricular themes in the identification and communication of values;

   - the *Informal Curriculum* refers to areas and aspects of school life outside of the classroom - extra-curricular activities such as sports, music, drama and school trips, discipline and pastoral care policies. It also includes issues and activities relating to the playground and the school's physical environment;

   - the *Hidden Curriculum* has a rather imprecise meaning and has been described by writers as "highly ambiguous" (Meighan 1981:52). While the Formal Curriculum and Informal Curriculum refer to quite definitive areas of the school, the hidden curriculum may cover aspects of both, while also relating to separate issues. For the purposes of this research the term is employed to indicate decisions, behaviours, and activities which may go unnoticed or unrecognised, but which may have considerable effect on the school community.

2. The Developmental Framework

   is based on the developmental dimensions of the Northern Ireland Curriculum, that is, values as they are associated with physical, intellectual, moral, cultural, spiritual and additionally emotional and social development. During the interviews there were some occasions when it was quite difficult to differentiate between value 'types' or to confidently class a value as, for example spiritual or emotional. It may be that the reader disagrees at times with the 'category' to which a value has been assigned.

Teachers did deliberate at times over this dilemma, but for the purposes of the research, it seemed more important to ascertain respondents' acknowledgement and recognition of values, than to quibble over the category to which a value should be assigned. Therefore there may be some overlaps in perceived values and a small degree of inconsistency in the identification of values.

3. The Context-Dependent Framework

refers to sets of values which arise from the distinctive character or location of the school. Factors may include the ages, ability, culture or social background of pupils and may be influenced or determined by views and expectations of parents, staff, pupils and members of the wider community.

The Developmental and Context-Dependent frameworks will be used to give greater definition and detail to values and in particular, to illustrate how they emerge within the settings of the classroom and school.

The Formal Curriculum

To undertake a systematic review of values in the formal curriculum, interviews focused on the Areas of Study within the Northern Ireland Curriculum, that is:

English
Mathematics
Science and Technology
Creative and Expressive Studies
Environment and Society, and
Language Studies.

Religious Education (RE) and Personal and Social Education (PSE) were also included. Cross-curricular themes featured throughout the discussions, although these have been presented separately following a review of the areas of study. Values were approached in the first instance through the Areas of study, by asking teachers about the values that could be identified and communicated through their teaching of individual subjects. Questions also addressed the permeation of the cross-curricular themes and associated values through the areas of study.

Although values in the formal curriculum were raised in interviews within the broader context of the areas of study, teachers' main point of reference (in the post-primary context) was invariably the subject which they taught. This is perhaps unsurprising, however it was interesting to observe at times, how vague any links with other subjects in an area of study appeared to be. Some teachers seemed clearly constrained by what are apparently definitive subject boundaries. Primary teachers did not communicate the same compartmentalised view of the primary curriculum and the lines of demarcation between subjects appeared to be less distinct and discernible.

Teachers' responses to the prevalence of values and value-related issues in their subjects, and their understanding, interpretation and communication of such issues are documented under each of the areas of study. Also the review of values in each area of study is not intended as an exhaustive analysis of every possible value connotation or reference, but rather as a reflective overview as presented by the respondent.

The majority of respondents are currently Education and Library Board Officers, occupying an advisory and support role. However, because they based their responses on their own teaching experiences, as well as the teachers they support all respondents in the main, are referred to as teachers. The use of *italics* in the main body of the text in this chapter indicates comments made by teachers.

English

English has been perceived as "an instrument of personal growth" (Bullock Report 1975:4) and as a means of equipping pupils with skills and abilities that will *"stand them in good stead right across and up through the curriculum."* Teachers were able to discuss values in relation to the English programmes of study with considerable insight and understanding. The values dimension seemed to be clarified further as discussions took place and teachers often spoke of *"making the connection"* once they had been given time to think.

Many respondents tended to look at English under the two headings of Language and Literature and from this perspective they were able to elicit examples of physical, intellectual, social, emotional, spiritual moral and cultural values.

English Language

- The ability to use language effectively at all stages of development was seen to encourage pupils to express themselves eloquently, to function independently and to increase their understanding, empathy and confidence.

- Some teachers referred to the physical, social and emotional value of creativity in language and the opportunities which were presented for pupils to deal with their thoughts and emotions, to improve their powers of expression and to develop their self-esteem. Teachers did admit however, that they were often *"itching to get their hands on children's work"*, in order to make corrections, revisions or changes. It was suggested that teachers sometimes needed to accept children's creativity as their own and not to interfere. Creative writing was also identified as a means of encouraging and developing a pupil's sense of autonomy, responsibility and self-control. Teachers also defined the approach to creative writing as a *"drafting"* approach where pupils are engaged in a revising and redrafting process until they produced an acceptable version.

- Primary teachers reported the *"sheer delight and enthusiasm"* shown by pupils at Key Stages 1 and 2 when reading aloud to the class or telling a story. They underlined the social and intellectual value of this activity, as well as its enjoyment and developmental value. Many individuals remarked on the *"onslaught of inhibition"* and the changing attitudes to reading aloud and personal expression as children progressed through the education system. Teachers spoke of some pupils' reluctance to read poetry or express an opinion, *"they just clam up"* and *"they get embarrassed"*. Opportunities for talking and listening were perceived as a valuable social and emotional aspect of English, encouraging children to empathise, share and respect others' perspectives.

- Some respondents refered to the disruption in pupils' development during the transfer between primary and post-primary schools and how teachers sometimes assume *"they are dealing with blank slates"* in Year 8. Post-primary teaching makes little reference to primary learning and therefore gives little in the way of acknowledgement to the value of primary experiences. English teachers talked of a *"creativity gap"* between primary and post-primary and a change in pupil's perceptions of and responses to the various components of English.

English Literature

• Reference was made to a continuing emphasis on literature in the curriculum and the consequent detrimental effects on language and in particular grammar development. Despite the oral component at GCSE, and the need for preparation in this area, teachers frequently observed that *"greater value is perceived in reading and the critical analysis of literature"*. In the post-primary context, more time was therefore given to examining texts and some teachers commented that a discussion or critique of a text was often undertaken on paper and not entered into through any kind of class discussion. This perception of a neglect of oral skills was mentioned by many teachers across all subject areas. Respondents spoke of a *"chalk and talk"* pedagogy associated with many subjects areas which eroded opportunities for pupil participation. This point is also made in the Northern Ireland Cohort Study where teachers commented that *"pupils [do] too much written work"* to the detriment of the "development of thought, self-expression, and communication with others".

(Harland et al, 1996:44)

• At Key Stages 3 and 4, the study of characters in novels was perceived as giving pupils the opportunity to explore feelings of empathy, sympathy and tolerance as well as *"to get in touch with themselves"*. Many texts were cited as examples to illustrate opportunities where teachers felt they could explore moral, social, emotional, spiritual and cultural issues. Interestingly, teachers who had studied these texts often had not considered their use in explicit *"value-terms"*.

• The choice of text for study at any stage in English was considered a moral and social values statement. Several teachers suggested that the *"choice of examination texts reflects values that are prevalent in society - avoiding direct language, uncomfortable incidents and other cultures"*. This point was reflected in some teachers' reactions to holding class discussions and dealing with controversial issues. They admitted they would find this *"too difficult and confrontational"*. Other teachers concluded that it was important to deal with cultural and moral values if it was relevant and appropriate to do so.

• Value was attached to the *"recursive nature of English"* where the nature of learning is essentially the same at every stage. Teachers commented that the same skills are applied and the same processes are at work.

Teachers felt that this enables pupils of all abilities to contribute in class and to experience some sense of achievement. One teacher commented, *"I find that no matter what level the child is at, they always have something to offer"*.

Conclusion

One teacher commented that *"you can never measure the impression a poem or text has made on a child - the value of the experience may only emerge years later"*. All teachers of English interviewed as part of the research concluded that values are scattered widely throughout the programmes of study and there are numerous opportunities to explore values through language, literature, creative writing and class discussions. Several drew particular attention to teachers' propensity to focus on cultural and moral issues as these were the *"most obvious places to find values"*.

Mathematics

Values and Mathematics were clearly not perceived to be close relations by many teachers. Initially, several declared Mathematics to be value-free and others suggested that any connections were artificial and contrived. Through discussions however, it became clear that there were actually some very interesting *"connections"*. Wilson (1981) lists over 200 references of studies examining the interaction between Mathematics and its cultural content. Many of these address the value systems implicit in those contents. (Tomlinson and Quinton 1986).

Mathematics and itellectual values

- Mathematics is universally regarded as an important subject which bestows a high intellectual value on it. Schools and parents attribute a high priority to Mathematics and this is widely recognised by pupils, many of whom feel under some considerable pressure to perform well and attain good examination results. Teachers frequently commented on this pressure and the fear which many children have of Mathematics. One teacher, whose school had undertaken a survey of pupils' perceptions of subjects, reported that Maths is *"the most hated and feared of all"*. Because of the high status of the subject many children are afraid *"of being left behind"* and of *"suffering embarrassment by having to go back to basics"*.

Teachers also pointed to *"harmful competitive elements"* which surround pupils and how these could seriously damage their self-confidence and progress in the subject. They concluded that this approach to Mathematics projected a strong set of intellectual, moral and cultural values which could have profound effects on pupils' learning and self-confidence.

Mathematics and methodology

• The methodology used in teaching Mathematics was identified as indicative of the values associated with the subject. Teachers commented that it was easier to instil enthusiasm and a positive attitude in pupils at primary school as they used many more practical and innovative teaching methods. One post-primary teacher commented *"it's all book work when you get to secondary so if you aren't interested in Maths in P7, you definitely won't be when you come here"*.

Teachers did agree in the main, that their approach to teaching the subject could communicate certain values. One teacher admitted, *"I know if I talk and direct all the time, I feel I take all the responsibility for the pupils' progress, so I try to have some pair or group work... to let them use their judgement and have some control over their progress and development"*.

Examples used in mathematics

• Teachers were asked to consider the content of Mathematics, in particular the choice of examples and problems featured in textbooks and exam papers. They then discussed and identified the sorts of moral, social and even political values which they felt were conveyed through these examples. Some teachers referred to Key Stage 3 and 4 materials which included graphs and charts presenting profit margins, production output and stock market figures. One teacher commented *"You know, I hadn't really thought about the nature of the data before, but ....it does clearly applaud capitalism and the struggle for wealth"*.

Research into the connection between Mathematics and the development of materials with alternative values is currently underway in England. These materials focus on data generated from other sources, reflecting a wider range of statistics related to social concerns, such as charity donations, road safety and environmental campaigns.

The relevance of Mathematics

- Teachers in post-primary schools frequently spoke of their attempts to communicate the relevance of Mathematics to society in general. They referred to the intellectual and social values of the subject which not only allowed pupils to solve mathematical-related problems, but also equip them with analytical, problem-solving and decision-making skills and curious and creative minds. A teacher observed, *"Maybe if pupils could see some value in Maths beyond knowing how to count and multiply and pass exams, they would enjoy it better"*.

Mathematics and 'perserverance', 'truth' and 'autonomy'

- Several primary teachers drew attention to the *"perseverance dimension"* of Mathematics, pointing to a perception that the subject required more persistence and application than others. Although many less able pupils found Mathematics difficult, they commented that any progress was considered to be an even greater achievement and *"cause for celebration"*. Perseverance was identified as a valuable personal quality which contributes greatly towards a pupil's character development. Similar points were raised in relation to girls' perceptions of and performance in Mathematics. The male-dominated image of Maths was also debated in relation to cultural and social values which teachers felt could influence commonly held attitudes towards the expectations of boys' and girls' performances in the subject.

- Some teachers felt that mathematics demonstrated certain inherent truths and that the subject had potential to promote this moral value in pupils' work and behaviour.

- One teacher also suggested that Mathematics could help pupils discover their autonomy, *"My GCSE pupils know that Maths is either right or wrong and that they can eventually find out for themselves ... they don't always need me"*.

Conclusion

Teachers concluded that it was easier to inspire pupils and to realise value-related aims and objectives for learning at primary school. They talked of post-primary pupils identifying *"negative values"* in Mathematics and of having already decided that they disliked or performed badly in the subject by the time they reach Year 8. It is interesting that many secondary school teachers echoed the view that, *"a lot of the first years tell me either explicitly or by their attitudes that they have already written Maths off. Some never give it a chance"*.

Most Mathematics teachers were interested in the concept of values and Mathematics, though some felt there was a danger in overplaying an affective values-link and making inappropriate connections.

Science and Technology

Initial reactions to a review of values underlying Science met with a diversity of responses from primary and post-primary teachers:

Science is neutral - it doesn't have any values.

Science is about things not people.

Teachers pay lip service to the proposition that science is value-laden. The fact is there isn't time to explore peripheral issues.

Teachers commented on many aspects of Science in the curriculum including the changes in curriculum structure and content; the challenges and difficulties of catering for all pupils; and the primary teacher's perception of Science. Clearly, teachers were much more in tune with the cognitive aspects of science (the knowledge and understanding of scientific laws; the attainment of skills for designing and undertaking investigative experiments) than with the affective or value-related dimensions.

From the interviews, individuals intimated that teacher training emphasised cognitive development and knowledge-based teaching at the expense of the human dimension (though this is an observation which is not exclusive to Science). Teachers demonstrated some difficulty in identifying examples of values within the Science and Technology curriculum. Technology teachers made similar remarks, but also mentioned the need for more emphasis on moral values, environmental issues and their implications for pupils to be considered at teacher training level.

Science and physical development

- In Science, primary teachers referred to the physical values which underpin studies of physical and psychological development. They illustrated these values by outlining some of the areas dealt with at Key Stages 1 and 2. Issues such as how the body works; how we move; the effects of exercise; how our bodies change; what we eat and wear, were all shown to promote pupils' understanding of their bodies and the importance of looking after themselves. Indeed physical values continued to pervade the Science curriculum right up to GCSE, with topics such as sex education, drug abuse and nutrition.

When sex education was raised in interviews, all the respondents except one commented that science teachers adopted a purely scientific approach and that the social, emotional and moral values which were associated with this topic were dealt with elsewhere.

I only deal with the plumbing. Other aspects are dealt with in PSE or HE. I'm not really qualified to deal with all that bit.

The RE teacher is really good at discussing those sorts of things.

There is a sort of party line. Science teachers leave those elements to the experts, the RE, HE and PSE teachers.

However alongside these comments, Science teachers acknowledged that they saw changes in their role, admitting that they had other issues to deal with aside from delivering the curriculum,

I think we are dealing with the social work aspects of teaching on a daily basis. Sometimes you've got to deal with the social aspects before you can progress to the knowledge and content.

Science and social and technological advancement

- Physical and moral values were also raised in the context of scientific and technological advances which are seen to be affecting humans, animals and the environment on a local, national or global scale. A teacher pointed to a fundamental effect which technology has had on human life through the use of medical and bio-technological techniques,

We are now redefining common terms like birth, parenthood and death. Technological advances are changing our perceptions and expectations regarding conception, suffering and death.

The moral, social and physical implications of various actions were discussed in relation to how they were introduced in the curriculum. Teachers referred to issues which they dealt with at various Key Stages which considered moral, physical and social values (animal extinction, wastage disposal, pollution, drug addiction, genetic engineering, medical advances, and nuclear technology). One teacher mentioned having discussed the concepts of risk and safety in decision-making concerning these issues. He pointed to the moral values implicit in the decision-making process. Cotgrove highlights this point when he states that, "Risk is not just a statistical calculation. It is also a moral judgement about defensible conduct" (Cotgrove 1981:pp124-5).

Primary Science

• In addressing pupils' earliest experiences of Science and Technology, teachers noted the importance of anchoring these subjects in the reality of pupils' everyday experiences. Primary teachers referred to activities which encourage children to examine the simplest pieces of technology they come into contact with. At Key Stage 1 pupils are also introduced to the effects of science and technology on society through such topics as 'transport' and 'the home' and through their introduction to computers.

Older pupils may consider *"how science shapes our lives"* and the limitations of science and technology to solve cultural problems. Science advisors referred to primary teachers as the *"unsung heroes"* in teaching Science. It was suggested that without any specialist training many teachers had come to terms with the requirements of the primary science curriculum, although considerable numbers still lacked confidence.

Technology teachers referred to opportunities for pupils to be creative and co-operative in processes which develop their sensitivities to other people's needs and cultures. A few respondents commented on the effectiveness of an historical approach which highlights how changes in cultural, moral and social values have been affected by science and technology.

Science and female pupils

- A value-related aspect of discussions concerning Science and Technology included the relationship between these subjects and female pupils. One teacher was forthright in summarising his opinion of girls' performances in Science,

  Girls and Science are just not compatible. Feelings and sensitivity are not needed for Science. Perhaps I shouldn't say it, but some girls would be better off in Home Economics.

  Other teachers commented that Science continued to be regarded as a *"male dynasty"* and that some teachers were *"still concerned about gender issues"*. The majority of teachers remarked that the perception that girls tended to perform less well in Science was not always true and that the attitude and approach of the individual teacher could have a profound effect on girls' confidence and progress.

Distinctions between grammar and secondary schools

- One grammar school teacher indicated his position regarding Science and less able pupils,

  I think it's a waste of time having those children attempt Science. Those single, double, triple award courses are no good if the kids want to do 'A' level. They haven't had anywhere near enough preparation.

  In response to this comment, a secondary teacher suggested that some grammar teachers felt the changes in the curriculum had left Science very *"diluted and weak."*

- A few grammar school teachers identified pressures which they felt from senior management and parents to achieve good GCSE and 'A' level results. They commented that sometimes it was *"like processing kids on to the next stage with as much in their heads as possible"*. Another stated, *"It's like stuffing cushions - in the hope that as much information as possible will stay there"*. Finally, one teacher confided, *"I do all the difficult stuff from September to Halloween so I sift out the ones who can't keep up"*. He maintained he was not the only teacher to do this.

- Other teachers commented that quite a few pupils were *just* managing to keep abreast of what was happening in class. *"In Science there is the odd high-flier. Most children are just keeping up".* These comments exposed strongly-held attitudes and values on the part of teachers and it would be interesting to ascertain if these values are apparent in the classroom and to what extent pupils may be aware of them.

Conclusion

In most cases teachers were willing to acknowledge and identify values implicit in Science. Most also felt they had dealt with values in some way through their teaching, though some admitted they do not normally frame their teaching in terms of values, *"You never stop to think, you just do".* Others acknowledged the importance of *"doing values",* but concluded, *"If there was more time, I think more teachers would deal with these additional areas".*

Home Economics

Home Economics (HE) was clearly perceived by other teachers to be *"awash"* with opportunities in the programmes of study to confront and explore values. For this reason it seemed more appropriate to deal with HE as a distinct area of interest. HE was identified as one of the pre-dominant value dimensions in the formal curriculum (along with PSE and RE) and so many elements of the programmes of study seemed entirely value-laden.

Home economics and the family

- HE teachers themselves agreed that the two strands of 'Family Life' and 'Home and Family Issues' consisted of many examples of moral, cultural, social, emotional and physical values. A third strand, 'Diet and Health' offers endless opportunities to examine physical and mental development, addressing for example, self-image, food preparation and diet-related health disorders.

- The changes and challenges facing the family in the 1990's moving towards the year 2000, was an issue raised by every teacher interviewed. Numerous sub-issues, including divorce, single parents, abortion, elderly parents and disability were identified during the course of interviews. There are further opportunities for the discussion of values through the study of family structures and units, employment, care, relationships and responsibilities. Teachers commented on the sensitivity and relevance of these issues for many pupils at a personal level and suggested the need for caution and diplomacy,

It is sometimes difficult to identify a context in which to broach these sorts of issues. You have to be so careful.

The good teacher is in tune with every pupil's learning and experiences. She is perceptive and sensitive.

The majority of teachers seemed to have responded well to curriculum changes, which as described by one individual, *"represented a tremendous shift in emphasis and change in content"*. There were some suggestions that this shift had improved the image of the subject, and more senior managers were giving it greater priority in the timetable.

Home economics and emotive issues

• Many of the issues related to family and relationships give rise to concerns about the management of feelings and emotional responses. For example, the HE programme states that pupils should have opportunities to consider stress and conflict and to identify strategies to cope with conflict. Examples of situations given include parent/child disagreements; family expectations; and the impact of traditional attitudes and beliefs on relationships. Teachers again emphasised the need to get to know the class well, in order to communicate confidently and to deal with issues effectively. They also referred to the importance of establishing a process for pupils to think about issues; demonstrating how to assemble and use information; analyse viewpoints; adopt and share their own personal viewpoints; and then make decisions about appropriate action. Teachers noted that by developing this knowledge pupils could apply it to many life situations and experiences into adulthood.

Conclusion

Teachers identified the values dimension as a major strength of Home Economics. As well as the knowledge and skills which are readily applicable to all aspects of life, they observed that pupils were given opportunities to develop their own personal values and attitudes; to identify personal strengths and weaknesses; and to identify goals and expectations for their futures.

Language studies

The language teachers interviewed as part of the project taught a combination of French, German, Spanish and Irish. The advisors were also able to comment on Italian, Russian and Japanese because of their contact with other teachers. When it came to examining values however the individual characteristics of a language were not a major consideration. It became clear that the teaching and learning processes of language development were remarkably similar. The initial responses from most teachers concerned examples of the exploration of cultural values which takes place as part of the teaching of foreign languages. Teachers also provided thoughtful insights into values involved in the processes of language teaching and learning.

Language and culture

• The programmes of study at Key Stage 3 and 4 state that pupils should have opportunities to develop an "understanding and appreciation of culture of the country or community of the target language. By identifying similarities and differences between cultures, they may learn to examine their own more objectively".

Teachers frequently drew attention to this statement and indicated different types of classroom activity which they undertook to fulfil these aims. Several teachers commented on the close relationship which exists between language and culture noting that, *"language and culture go hand in hand."* They indicated that it is virtually impossible to learn another language and not have *"some grasp of what the culture is about"*. Teachers pointed out that in learning about other cultures, pupils also learn about their own. It was claimed that this sort of experience promotes tolerance in that, *"it gives a different perspective on Northern Ireland"* and *"it helps open their minds"*.

Languages and social development

• Teachers mentioned a range of opportunities where language studies could contribute to the social development of pupils, for example, by encouraging self-confidence and providing pupils with *"the chance to express themselves"*. Regular group interaction and working in pairs also promoted the development of sensitive talking and listening skills which teachers concluded were readily transferable across the curriculum,

If you can get them to really listen to their partner, and it is possible, you know they are on their way to developing a very valuable and valued skill.

Languages and moral issues

* Opportunities to introduce and explore moral values were perceived to be more limited. Teachers reported that issues with moral undercurrents did arise from time to time, though the nature of the materials in use in schools often did not place a great deal of emphasis on this aspect of development. With increased access to videos, magazines and newspapers, pupils were coming into contact with *"undiluted moral material"*. However it was stated that pupils often did not have sufficient knowledge and understanding of the language to read or discuss such issues and for this reason teachers do not always consider such material appropriate. Pupils at 'A' level may be presented with more opportunities to address the moral aspects of language through set texts and news materials.

Languages and strategies for less able pupils

* Language teachers made several comments concerning their approach with pupils who experience difficulties with language studies. Some outlined strategies and tasks which acknowledged and rewarded a pupil's achievements. Reference was frequently made to the *"creative teacher"* who was able to develop and implement motivating activities. One teacher also referred to the difficulties of pitching language lessons at an appropriate level for the whole class,

    The challenge is to target lessons at the top end to promote development and at the bottom end to give encouragement. Too often lessons tend to hit around the middle.

    Interviews with special needs teachers revealed a debate concerning the value of language studies for pupils with moderate learning difficulties. Some felt it gave children an opportunity to experience part of the statutory curriculum and to revisit the grammar and components of English, while others thought it was not particularly relevant or should be an *"optional extra"*.

    Another challenge identified in language teaching was to enthuse the disinterested, disenchanted pupil. Teachers referred to the importance of choosing a good selection of resources and using a wide variety of methods.

Conclusion

An over-riding concern of language teachers was to capitalise on opportunities to consider social and moral issues where they arise naturally within the context of language teaching, rather than in an contrived way.

Advisors also reported different approaches to language studies in secondary and grammar schools. They suggested that pupils in secondary schools tended to be encouraged to enjoy and appreciate a language while grammar school choices of a language were often based on strategic choice as an examination subject selection or the prospects of a successful grade at GCSE.

Creative And Expressive Studies

According to teachers engaged in the area of Creative and Expressive studies many aspects of the subjects included under this umbrella term are the *"epitome"* of physical, cultural, spiritual, moral, social and emotional values. Teachers frequently identified the salient features of Art and Design, Drama, Media Studies, Music and Physical Education (PE) in affective, attitudinal and value-related terms.

Perceptions of Creative and Expressive Studies

• Teachers observed that it was precisely because of the irrefutable *"value characteristics"* that Creative and Expressive studies occupied a *"subordinate"* and *"inferior"* position within the curriculum. Teachers remarked on a bias within the curriculum on cognitive development resulting *inter alia* in a neglect of the affective and creative side. Several respondents alluded to the potentially negative consequences of this type of curriculum on children's futures in the adult world,

  Eminent educationalists and business people like Sir John Harvey-Jones are pointing out that it is no longer just enough to be good at the knowledge-based subjects or the skill-oriented subjects. The demand is now for people to be innovative and creative, therefore the particular skills developed in the creative and expressive area are all important.

Society is now looking for people who think, not just say and do. Yes it is important to have skills but you must also be able to address problems, know how to deal with them and then solve them.

Creativity and physical development

- All the Creative and Expressive subjects yielded evidence of implicit and explicit values associated with the physical development of young people. In the context of physical development PE presented many opportunities for the promotion of co-ordination and movement skills, body awareness, physical and verbal interaction, physical expression and the development of personal qualities and attitudes. Primary teachers identified PE as a very appropriate vehicle for highlighting the value of exercise, hygiene and healthy eating. One teacher commented, *"it is generally setting children on the road to a healthy lifestyle"*. Other teachers referred to the far-reaching effects such education might have,

You hope that they might remember some of the things you tell them about food and exercise and that they might take it home with them.

I often tell them why we do PE I think teachers sometimes have to spell this out for them. Sometimes they don't hear it anywhere else.

Music, in particular the use of musical instruments and singing, was perceived to enhance a child's co-ordination and ability to control fine movements. This was an observation frequently made by special school teachers who commented on the tremendous opportunities it offered children with moderate and severe physical disabilities and learning difficulties to gain control of their bodies and to interact with instruments, space and each other.

Various activities in Art and Design were identified as having similar value - clay modelling, painting, drawing, creative tasks using textiles, and printing. In addition, many aspects of these subjects were seen to encourage co-operation, trust and perseverance.

Creative movement

- Teachers in primary and post-primary schools are being encouraged to introduce dance and creative movement in order to explore the more creative and expressive aspects of PE Dance and movement, like Drama are seen to develop children's awareness of their bodies, their powers of expression and their ability to explore feelings and emotions. A few teachers who had undertaken dance with their pupils thought that it was a refreshing change from games and sports activities. One teacher also said that, *"creative movement is where you might just find the non-academic child sparkling"*. Most teachers felt that dance was a bit too specialised and complex for the untrained while some post-primary male teachers thought it was *"out of the question really"*.

• The interviews uncovered a fairly widespread feeling amongst primary teachers concerning a lack of confidence and knowledge about PE. They frequently complained of a lack of training in PE and the small amount of time allocated to the subject in many schools. This point has been mentioned at a National level with comments about the "government's ostrich-like... attitude to the standard of PE in primary schools where more than 90% of teaching is carried out by non-specialists". The gravity of this situation has been set alongside evidence suggesting that,

the 7 to 11 age range establishes the attitudes, enthusiasm and basic capabilities in physical activity. By the age of 11 most children have sorted out their feelings about physical education and sport.

(Lee in TES October 1995:17)

Cultural influences in Creative and Expressive Studies

• Several primary teachers drew attention to the inclusion of traditional street games such as hopscotch and circle singing games in their PE programme. They explained the games were linked to geography or history topics on traditions and culture which were being studied concurrently. In music, teachers referred to background studies and pupils' experiences of music from other countries and cultures, such as North American Indians and 'the blues'. They also highlighted cultural elements in studies of the construction and composition of indigenous music and analyses of traditional and world music. One teacher commenting on culture and music said,

You find as you get to know the curriculum more that there are lots of opportunities to think about culture and it is better when you just find the connection, instead of forcing it.

- Areas for considering cultural and traditional values in Art and Design were highlighted by several post-primary teachers. They commented on the cultural, political and social values underpinning art masterpieces which were studied by pupils and the *"cultural baggage"* which pupils carry in *"designing their own masterpieces"*.

Exploring identity as part of Creative and Expressive Studies

- Within Media studies teachers reported that an exploration of identity was often at the heart of their work and provided a basis for classroom discussions about gender, stereotyping, nationality and religious identity. Drama was also perceived to provide pupils with effective tools to explore identity in a safe and supportive environment. Teachers mentioned various techniques such as role play, character shadowing and improvisation. Drama and media studies teachers endorsed the processes and structures available through drama for effective and productive studies of sensitive moral and controversial issues.

It allows pupils to express themselves without the constraints of language and it encourages kids to ask questions, challenge commonly-held views, and analyse messages in the media and modern popular culture.

Emotional development through Creative and Expressive studies

- There was a consensus amongst teachers of Creative and Expressive subjects that emotional values pervaded the entire area of study. PE teachers indicated that pupils' participation in dance facilitated interaction with emotions. Dance drama, creative dance and character dance were all seen as mechanisms which give pupils access to their own and others' feelings and experience in knowing how to interpret and manage these feelings. In Art and Design, teachers outlined opportunities for pupils to make personal and visual responses through design and construction and by accessing a wide range of stimuli, technique and media.

- In Music, pupils were encouraged to recognise the manipulative power of music and its ability to distort meaning and reality. Teachers commented that while sensitive issues might arise from time to time, they tended to be peripheral to the main objectives of lessons. Several teachers referred to the analyses of music from films such as 'Schindler's List' and 'West Side Story', but also added that they had not actively sought out opportunities to initiate discussions around any of the difficult or controversial issues addressed in these films.

- The processes of recognising, interpreting, accepting and managing emotions characterised many conversations where teachers referred to the powerful effects of images, words, sounds, music, mime, and silence. Another important emotional aspect of these subjects, mentioned by a few teachers, was the feelings aroused in pupils through performance. Pupil experiences of failure, success, rejection and injustice on the sports field, on the stage or in music was considered to have a potentially profound effect on their emotions. On the other hand, many activities in the Creative and Expressive subjects were considered to have an *"almost therapeutic effect"*, providing non-verbal mechanisms to communicate or heal personal emotional traumas.

- There were evidently many opportunities to explore and experience the emotional dimensions of these subjects, with or without the teacher's active involvement. A sizeable percentage of teachers still expressed some discomfort and reluctance in *"going too far"*, explaining how they preferred not to, *"get too deep into these emotional experiences"*. Their fears focused around their inability to deal with emotional traumas that could arise and the repercussions of becoming involved with sensitive situations, as one teacher said, regarding a third year Art and Design class,

It's not that you're not looking to help. You're just afraid in some cases, of what you might find.

Spiritual development through Creative and Expressive Studies

- Teachers strongly agreed that spiritual values underpinned many areas of the Creative and Expressive area of study, however they experienced some difficulties in articulating tangible examples. Many teachers felt that spiritual experiences and development are, by their very nature, ethereal and immeasurable. Such experiences were also considered to be intensely personal and individual and therefore it was not possible to recognise every spiritual element or encounter within the subjects. Responses from PE teachers tended to focus on dance as an expressive process. In Media Studies and Art, teachers indicated how words, graphics and images were employed as stimuli to provoke pupils into reflecting, analysing and questioning what they feel and believe. Music teachers used terms such as 'reflection', 'inspiration' and 'motivation' to describe the kinds of spiritual experience which might be evoked through different musical encounters. Art was identified as a powerful means to self-discovery by many teachers in both *"passive and active ways"*. Others referred to the subjects' *"aesthetic powers"* and the *"...opportunities for identifying and appreciating beauty, peace and joy"*. Drama was also seen to *"equip pupils with confidence and knowledge to undertake investigations into their beliefs, faith and principles"*.

Creative and Expressive studies and special needs

* Special school teachers clearly attached great value to the activities available to children through Creative and Expressive studies. Much emphasis was placed upon self-exploration and self-expression and encouraging children to participate with others in drawing, singing, movement and drama. Every special school visited during the project was making plans for, or engaged in rehearsals for a concert, play or musical show. All the schools had extensive displays of the children's art work in the reception areas, corridors and classrooms. Teachers indicated many positive effects on the children of their involvement in creative and expressive activities in developing qualities such as self-confidence, self-esteem, self-knowledge, self-control, responsibility, creativity and team spirit. Opportunities to express and explore their own personal problems or disabilities were also indicated. The advent of drama, art and music therapies have given greater emphasis to the healing powers in the arts, and provided opportunities in many special schools for the exploration of physical, emotional and spiritual experiences.

Assessment and Creative and Expressive Studies

* A number of teachers referred to assessment and the criteria they used in evaluating pupils' work for Art and Design and Music. The assessment of musical compositions was a particular example of teachers identifying the difficulties in assigning a value to pupils' work. While many respondents approved of guidelines which were issued for assessing composition, there were some teachers who acknowledged the validity of placing an intrinsic value in pupils' work (the notion of attributing subjective values to a piece of artwork or musical composition). A few teachers also referred to the sensitivity involved in offering any criticisms of pupils' creativity which was essentially a very personal matter.

The status of Creative and Expressive Studies

- A common issue raised by almost all the teachers interviewed was the approach adopted in schools for timetabling Creative and Expressive subjects. Teachers complained that these subjects were, *"slotted in wherever possible"* or *"left until the end with RE"*. Music teachers almost invariably commented that music was only *"important"*, *"worried about"*, or *"a priority"* when a school musical event was approaching. The rest of the time it was *"second rate"*, a *"lesser subject"* or *"bottom of the heap"*.

- Media Studies, according to many teachers, is poorly valued, particularly within grammar schools. Some secondary teachers concluded that *"grammar schools think it's a Mickey Mouse subject"*, or *"grammars don't think its a valid area for study"*. Media studies teachers in both secondary and grammar schools also reported some of their colleagues' perceptions as,

I suppose it's good for kids who won't do well anywhere else;

It's alright for the less-academic ones; and

Sure it only encourages them to watch more TV and do even less work.

Such perspectives left many Media Studies teachers feeling that their subject was at times *"fighting for its corner"* and some teachers had attempted to raise the status of their subject by initiating cross-curricular projects with English, Drama and History. This point is confirmed by the Northern Ireland Curriculum Cohort Study which suggests that,

teachers' concerns about the comparatively low status of the creative and expressive arts in the Northern Ireland Curriculum are forcefully corroborated by pupils' prima facie responses. (Harland et al, 1996:77).

- Drama teachers repeatedly drew attention to their subject as a potential vehicle for children to explore sensitive and controversial issues across the different areas of the curriculum. They indicated how, by using different drama techniques a teacher in almost any subject could develop children's abilities to understand and empathise with other positions and experiences. However, the responses from teachers of others subjects were somewhat less enthusiastic. They spoke of their inexperience, lack of skills and lack of confidence in the whole area typified by the comment, *"Maybe if I had some training I'd think about using drama from time to time"*.

• Comments were frequently made regarding the role of the Music, PE and Drama, and to a lesser degree Art and Design, as important elements in a school Public Relations (PR) strategies. These observations are addressed in greater detail under the Informal Curriculum.

Conclusion

Creative and Expressive subjects seemed to present teachers with many real and unique opportunities to highlight and explore different values. In doing so, some teachers acknowledged the potential for the establishment of more open and effective relationships between themselves and their pupils. Whilst others acknowledged this possibility, most also voiced strong concerns about maintaining *"appropriately distanced relationships"* and professional detachment.

Environment and Society

A comment from one primary school teacher seemed to summarise the perspectives of many teachers of this area,

> *Environment and Society is all about life and perhaps more accurately, living. I suppose when you talk about values, then it's looking at the values that brought us to where we are and the values that will take us forward. Its also about how we exist and interact with our many environments and neighbours.*

When asked to consider the current provision for values in History, Geography and Business Studies respondents immediately reflected on the opportunities to address cultural and moral values, particularly in History and Geography. Other values took a little longer to "tease" out, however the majority of teachers' responses did suggest that Environment and Society does embrace a wide range of physical, social, emotional, intellectual, moral and cultural values.

Values related to intellectual development

- Teachers valued 'intellectual development' in Environmental and Social Studies through the acquisition of knowledge and skills in this area. This encompassed the recognition and assimilation of new terminology such as treaty, politics, society, domestic and foreign policy, and conceptual knowledge relating to chronology, change, progression, and consequences in History. In Geography, teachers listed terms such as settlement, environment, pollution, economic development, population, latitude and longitude. In Business Studies they referred to pupils identifying the roles of citizens, consumers and employees.

Personal development through environmental and social studies

- In terms of physical values and in particular, personal qualities, all the subjects yielded opportunities for children to learn how to make choices and decisions, to participate effectively in group activities and to develop healthy and mature attitudes. History teachers underlined the importance of pitching their presentations of historical events at the appropriate age level. Several drew attention to the need to revise certain lessons, *"to ensure they were suitable for the target audience"*. One respondent commented how,

  third and fourth year boys have to be handled sensitively, they ... are sometimes still very immature and unable to deal effectively with some everyday issues.

- Also in relation to physical values, one teacher suggested that the power and potential impact of expressive and persuasive rhetoric and movement, demonstrated by famous orators such as Stalin, Hitler and Mussolini, might also constitute an interesting lesson. Pupils could analyse and discuss how and why these individuals succeeded in securing and maintaining power, as part of their studies of European, Fascist, or twentieth century dictatorships.

Social development through environmental and social studies

- In the context of the primary school, teachers identified many examples of opportunities to promote pupils' social development. They referred to lessons which focused on care of the environment and pets, learning about other people and relationships and cultivating respect for and understanding of different lifestyles. Pupils were using a variety of strategies to explore these areas, including pair and group work, active learning sessions, oral presentations and class exposition. A few post-primary teachers gave some concrete examples of undertaking a study of a plantation family in Ulster, in order to explore lifestyles and society at this time, while another illustrated a lesson studying slogans and the effect that these could have on communities, government policies and conflicts.

Values related to cultural identity and tradition

• Values related to cultural identity arose in many areas of the History programmes. At Key Stages 1 and 2 storytelling, myths and songs were recognised as a means of communicating the traditions which make up a society. Through Geography children learn, *"how to see themselves in relation to other children, other places and then other traditions".*

Teachers recognised how historical studies reflect many aspects of culture through studies at primary level of the home, play, school, transport and shopping. At post-primary level topics mentioned included politics, war, economics, social and educational policies. In undertaking a study of Northern Ireland culture by examining historical and political events one teacher commented,

I try to encourage the kids to see that there is more to this country than what you see in the media, hear from politicians or catch scribbled on a gable wall.

His point highlighted the role of History in raising sensitive and controversial issues using a variety of methods which encourage young people to examine and understand the values and beliefs of themselves and others.

Controversial issues

• Teachers of History commented on the controversial nature of many aspects of their programme of study the strong feelings, even uncontrolled outbursts, which arose especially in relation to Northern Ireland. One teacher suggested that,

History has a strange power to provoke a mixture of emotions in the classroom. Teachers have to quite resolutely put their feelings to the side and try to concentrate on presenting a clearly balanced perspective.

Other teachers pointed out how difficult this could be. Every teacher alluded to the sensitivities in teaching about Northern Ireland and to the fact that many children still lived in what are essentially divided communities.

Values and development education

• Examples provided by Geography teachers highlighted opportunities to explore the impact of decisions and actions on people and the environment. These included studies of homelessness, air and sea pollution, famine, land development programmes and profit markets. A common feature of such studies is that they draw attention to the value systems of others and pupils' personal beliefs and values in relation to the issues concerned.

Teachers demonstrated how by looking at environmental change, conflicts over resources or environmental management pupils are afforded opportunities to identify and analyse personal and corporate values and attitudes and to determine how these could influence subsequent judgements, consequences and actions. One particular topic which was frequently raised concerned perceptions of developing countries and how they are perceived. Teachers discussed the negative implications of ethnocentricity and the degree to which opinions and beliefs could be determined or altered by media images.

• Several teachers were working towards promoting positive images of children in countries characterised by famine, war, disease and death.

The TV images are not the whole story. We want to present the truth about these cultures. Yes, there are terrible scenes, but there are also other scenes, which children might even be able to identify with. The children in our pictures are wearing clothes, playing and eating dinner - not so different from our own pupils.

Their aim was to temper television images with equally real, but happier, healthier images of children in developing countries and to encourage pupils to develop a critical awareness of media images.

Values and Business Studies

• Business Studies presents pupils with an insight into business culture, providing opportunities to examine the structure and processes of business deals, contracts and interaction. Teachers commented on how pupils are also confronted, through different topics and assignments with various definitions of society's values such as enterprise, work, ambition, profit, and rewards. Recognition was given to teachers' responsibility to present such values, as one teacher said, *"in the broader context of things, alongside greater achievements like honesty, justice and respect"*. Other issues included the introduction of maternity and paternity leave, flexitime, and the rising number of female managers. Other aspects of gender issues in the workplace also featured in discussions and debates.

Morality and environmental and social studies

The interviews with teachers involved in environmental and social studies highlighted the extent to which this Area of Study can lead to an exploration of the morality of certain practices as well as a less subjective consideration of the values involved.

• In Geography, awareness and care of the local environment is addressed through numerous projects which raise questions about individual, collective and corporate responsibilities and the morality of various actions. One Geography teacher remarked that,

   pupils can step in and out of each actor's shoes and experience what's going on. It helps them to appraise a situation more fully and to understand the profound difficulties in identifying the "right" decision.

• In History the purpose and consequence of actions is considered through an interpretation of historical events which may include some understanding of the morality of other time periods and cultural settings.

• Teachers of Business Studies referred to elements of the programmes of study which address the characteristics of morally-correct business practice (honesty, fairness, justice and tolerance) and *"morally-corrupt"* practices (fraud, prejudice, dishonesty and exploitation). Other opportunities to address morality occur in the context of human rights issues relating to the working and employment conditions in various countries, fair pay and issues such as the exportation of live animals. Teachers related details of lively debates which had centred around several of these subjects.

Personal beliefs and attitudes

• A number of teachers referred to the capacity of their subject to challenge pupils' attitudes, beliefs, motives and values. For example, the study of various conflicts in History gives rise to moral complexities of cause and consequence and the positive and negative effects of change. Political and civil unrest in Northern Ireland was also a focus of study at Key Stage 4. Teachers communicated a range of perceptions regarding the difficulties of confronting and teaching these issues. Their experiences depended to a some degree on the location of their school and the background (and in some cases sex) of their pupils. One teacher remarked,

Dealing with these issues is like walking on a minefield. You have to try so hard to get the pupils to think about other people's feelings and opinions and not just their own. Human life, truth, and respect - for some of these kids, moral values like these just don't come into it.

Teachers, especially at the post-primary level acknowledged the moral dimension of many issues they mentioned, though the challenge to focus on them more explicitly for some, was just too difficult to meet.

Conclusion

Most teachers in the area of Environment and Society, referred to the *"power"* which resides with teachers to choose which topics to study. Some commented on the extent to which a teacher could distort situations and events. Most agreed that while very few teachers set out to deliberately indoctrinate pupils or promote propaganda in their teaching, teachers should be aware of the extent to which their teaching methods or selection of resources may introduce an issue from a particular perspective or bias. According to some it is difficult not to do this. The overriding message however was the need for teachers to be ever conscious of how they present information and what they perceive their pupils to understand by it.

Religious Education

Religious Education (RE) was indisputably the most commonly identified *"values dimension"* of the curriculum. Almost every teacher made some reference to this subject at some stage throughout the interviews. Some respondents also referred to the RE teacher as the *"values man"* or the *"moral expert"*, suggesting morals and values were *"his speciality"*. Teachers expressed a variety of opinions about RE. Some thought it provided pupils with a benefical departure from the pressures of the scientific and cognitive-based curriculum, *"giving their brains a rest"*. Others felt it was a valuable opportunity for pupils to gain further accreditation suggesting, *"it's more useful now that pupils are doing it at GCSE"*.

The RE syllabus places a significant emphasis on values, attitudes, beliefs and morals, particularly through the third part of the core syllabus entitled 'Morality'. The main aim of this course is stated as a preface to each Key Stage,

> pupils should develop their ability to think and judge about morality, to relate Christian moral principles to personal and social life and to identify values and attitudes that influence behaviour. (DENI 1993).

A review of the examples given in the programmes of study for each of the attainment target clearly outlines the permeation of physical, moral, cultural, emotional, social and spiritual values throughout the subject. These examples include a recognition and acceptance of self, a concern about the environment, management of relationships, decision-making and a respect for love and life.

Because the programmes of study embrace such a rich, eclectic range of value-related material, it seemed rather unnecessary to ask RE teachers to restate these during interviews. Instead, teachers were encouraged to focus on general perceptions and experiences of the RE programme, teaching methodologies and strategies and debates surrounding value-related issues within the subject. Additionally, because RE was widely perceived as the main context for the exploration and discussion of values, it was considered that a review of its status within the curriculum would be appropriate and enlightening.

RE as 'emotional cement'

*   Many of the teachers interviewed, drew attention to the valuable opportunities RE affords pupils to explore and discuss many issues which

have direct relevance for their own lives. Some teachers stated that RE was helpful in supporting *"sensitive"* aspects of their own subjects. Examples were given of the moral, social and emotional aspects of sex education which are often not addressed in Science and explorations of identity and tradition which support work in History and English. One RE teacher commented that RE was sometimes perceived as *"filling in gaps left by other subjects"* and another suggested that in addressing difficult or sensitive issues she was going where *"other teachers fear to tread"*.

The low status of RE

• Although the valuable contribution of RE to the curriculum was endorsed by many teachers and senior managers, RE teachers were concerned with the low status of the subject. They felt that this was due in part to the emphasis on knowledge and skills within the curriculum which is then embodied in the approach adopted by many schools. They indicated that while the content and teaching of RE was often applauded by head teachers and senior staff, it was often the last subject to be timetabled and the first to be changed or reduced in terms of the time allocated. Teachers spoke of RE being *"slotted in"* or *"tagged on"* the school timetable after every other subject.

Many also mentioned that a considerable proportion of RE teachers were non-specialists and that in many schools RE teaching was shared between several teachers, sometimes up to as many as eight. Many schools did not have an RE specialist. According to one RE teacher, *"other staff think there's nothing to it. It's just a matter of rattling through the facts"*. This issue has been raised in England and Wales with an OFSTED review "identifying a lack of specialist staff and a lack of commitment to the subject by school managers" (Pyke, TES 1995).

Several teachers also observed that despite the introduction of statutory requirements for Religious Education, parents and pupils perceived little value in studying the subject, if the school did not also offer some academic accreditation,

They've told me they think it's a waste of time unless they can get some sort of certificate. It's a terrible shame that this seems to be the only contribution RE can make.

RE, personal beliefs and commitment

- The personal beliefs of RE teachers were also mentioned by teachers in terms of their perception and delivery of the subject. In 1994, SCAA established several working groups to identify the content of model RE syllabi. The conclusion reached by these groups led SCAA to state that RE *"can only be understood and learnt from within"* and also that *"religion can only be taught from within - that is with a religious commitment"* (Wilson, TES 1995). RE teachers who were interviewed, considered whether RE teaching was approached any differently or if there was anything *"lacking"* if the teacher was not an *"actively committed Christian"*. The variety of responses included the following:

While the non-Christian teacher may be very thorough, honest and interested, there are some things that will not be conveyed.

The Christian teacher will communicate the real meaning and experience of prayer. The non-Christian will not.

Many of the values in RE are common to society - honesty, fairness, tolerance and kindness - a teacher doesn't need a religious commitment to teach these.

A good background knowledge and enthusiasm for RE is enough.

Respondents frequently referred to the RE teacher who displayed strong, unshakeable convictions and the temptation to use RE lessons as an opportunity to proselytise. There was a unanimous rejection of any teacher forcing their views on pupils or teaching from *"a high moral ground"*. A good RE teacher was characterised as caring, tolerant, interested and empathic, with an enthusiasm for the subject and a good working knowledge of the course contents.

RE, values education and moral education

- The notion of 'values education' arose quite naturally in some conversations and several teachers went so far as to suggest that RE involves a broadly similar approach when dealing with complex and emotional issues. The distinguishing characteristic of RE was that the morality it promotes stems from a strong spiritual basis and a definitive biblical influence. A number of teachers expressed reservations about the term 'morality' because of its negative associations with rules, prohibitions and judgment. In general, teachers felt the salient point was how morality was approached and explored in class and to what extent pupils found it interesting, relevant and challenging. One respondent commented that, *"it is important to acknowledge the value differences across generations,"* while another concluded that, *"there are basic values that don't go out of fashion"*.

* Many individuals commented on morality and debated its definition. There was a concern that the issues involved should not be defined too narrowly. *"Its not just sexuality, you know"* was one response and another teacher stated emphatically that the *"stereotypical moral issues - sex, abortion and suicide are only part of the story"*. These statements corroborated others' views that the term had a much broader meaning. Teachers commented that morality dealt with, *"the big issues - life, death, relationships, fears, feelings"*, with *"love, justice and life"* and *"guiding pupils to understand, to make choices and to stand up for what they believe"*. On no occasion did teachers echo a perceived motivation behind the RE syllabus in England and Wales, *"the belief that young people must be taught how to be good"* (Wilson, TES 1995). Indeed many teachers expressed some concern that to adopt a deterministic approach, concentrating explicitly on definitions of 'right' and 'wrong' would be damaging to the whole spiritual and emotional content of RE. They were anxious that,

RE would then be subsumed under moral education and we would be reduced to teaching what is right and wrong.

Clearly, teachers regarded the morality dimension of RE from a much broader, more inclusive perspective, placing a strong emphasis on the value of each individual, their understanding and opinion, and their participation in contemporary society. It was also evident that teachers valued the developmental aspect of RE, commenting on the crucial opportunities which the programme of study offered young people to reflect on, and shape their views and opinions. One teacher remarked,

While pupils will never have to deal with many issues in their subjects again, the issues in RE will continue to crop up again and again.

Teaching methods and strategies in RE

- RE teachers frequently reiterated how the choice of appropriate and imaginative teaching methods and strategies, and the development of an *"open, honest and accepting relationship with pupils"*, are crucial for effective teaching. Several commented that an essential part of discussion work is the opportunity for pupils to give their own perspective and to examine where their own values had originated.

RE in controlled and maintained schools

- Teachers in maintained post-primary schools mentioned the benefits of retreats for Years 11 and 12, where pupils are given the opportunity to spend time together away from the classroom to discuss a wide range of issues, *"usually including relationships and sexuality"*. One teacher felt that *"taking children out of the timetabled routine and exam-oriented atmosphere"* gives pupils the opportunity to *"think more freely and speak more openly about real life issues"*. A few teachers commented how the maintained school approach to RE was less 'formalised' than in controlled schools and that the teaching made greater reference to marginalised groups such as travellers, alcoholics and the poor. Another teacher suggested there was less concern for *"outcasts"* in the controlled schools approach.

- In terms of the values underpinning the approach to RE in the controlled and maintained sectors almost every individual interviewed suggested there is a difference between the two, though they often experienced some difficulty in articulating the distinctions. Many teachers suggested that because Catholic liturgy and ideals pervaded much of the daily life of maintained schools, RE was a more *"natural"* and integral part of pupils' education. (The concept of a Catholic School ethos is referred to in Chapter six). In addition where schools had strong links with a local Catholic parish and clergy this was perceived to raise the profile of RE within the school. In controlled schools pupils are drawn from a range of denominations and none and this is reflected in a broader based 'non-confessional' approach to RE. One respondent suggested that teachers and pupils in controlled schools experience RE through *"words and understanding"*, but often displayed a *"lack of heart"*. In maintained schools, on the other hand, teachers and pupils *"have meaningful experiences"*, but are *"often unable to articulate their theology"*.

RE and integrated schools

• Integrated schools have designed RE programmes to meet the needs of Catholic and Protestant pupils within their enrolment. In most cases this has meant identifying a common programme augmented by provision for specific denominational needs. In drafting and implementing an RE programme in integrated schools, teachers spoke of *"starting from a point of contact and sharing experience, while still using the core syllabus"*. An integrated primary school teacher commented that, *"the staff didn't realise how much they had in common until they started thinking about basic values and beliefs"*. Several teachers in the integrated sector said that they felt more motivated about RE than some of their counterparts in mainstream schools,

Its so much more exciting and pupils greet each others differences with interest and acceptance.

An important point emerging from discussions with teachers was that in the integrated sector RE is based on the premise that children need to feel sure of their own tradition before they can share this tradition with others. For some teachers this added an additional impetus for integrated schools to ensure that each child is well-acquainted with their own religious background and tradition.

Conclusion

The extent to which RE may contribute to pupil development and the wider curriculum was perceived to be largely dependent on the respect and support accorded the subject by the senior management in individual schools. Many RE teachers felt that the subject had more to offer but two or three periods a week was limiting, *"Given respect, there are many areas of the curriculum which the RE teacher can broach and deal with quite effectively"*.

Some teachers acknowledged a definite improvement in the status of the subject. They suggested that this may be because schools are discovering that more and more *"outside issues"* are creeping into the classroom and teachers are increasingly pressed to repond to these. One teacher concluded, *"RE is the Cinderella subject, but it seems it's now perhaps getting ready for the ball"*.

Personal and Social Education

Personal and Social Education (PSE) was widely recognised as strongly values-oriented. Teachers in many areas of study described the content of PSE as *"heavily value-based"*, commenting on the contribution it could potentially make towards the affective and behavioural development of pupils. The notion of 'development' was prominent in many discussions, as teachers commented on opportunities for "moral development", "emotional development" and "personal and social" development. When pressed to offer a more detailed analysis of these terms some teachers acknowledged that they would have difficulty since they often used the terms interchangeably. Whilst such descriptors are used widely it appears that teachers have had limited opportunity to unravel or discuss the distinctions and nuances of the terms.

Values and attitudes involved in PSE

- Teachers indicated that many facets of PSE addressed values, such as personal attitudes and beliefs, self-knowledge, interpersonal relationships and decision-making. PSE, according to teachers gives pupils the opportunity to leave the usual knowledge-based, intellectual dimension of the curriculum to one side and to concentrate on their *"social, personal, moral, sexual and emotional selves"*. Teachers pointed out that in this sense PSE is unique, allowing pupils of all abilities to develop and achieve. They also drew attention to opportunities to examine cultural values, giving examples of where teachers could consider the concepts of identity and tradition which encourages pupils to develop an empathic understanding of other views and beliefs.

Learning in partnership

- The controversial and sensitive nature of many of the issues encountered in PSE had prompted many teachers to adopt teaching approaches which facilitate collaboration and joint-participation of teachers and pupils. Several teachers spoke of aiming to achieve *"a sense of equal status between teacher and class"* so that pupils might develop a strong sense of ownership and partnership about their own learning. For this approach to be successful teachers recognised that they had to be prepared to *"share, perhaps even expose a part of their inner selves"* and to *"trust and invest some faith in the class"*.

PSE as 'education for life'

• Teachers commented that in common with RE, PSE is a form of *"life education"*, that is, education which will potentially inform and guide pupils in their decisions, opinions and behaviour for the rest of their lives. From this perspective, PSE was defined as an essentially "pragmatic" subject - guiding, preparing, training, and equipping pupils to engage effectively in inter-personal relationships and to *"participate actively in daily living"*. Teachers went on to refer to the many diverse pressures which exist in modern society and to the concerns that pupils will grow up to function in this society at an unthinking and perfunctory level. Equipping pupils with the knowledge and skills to implement thinking and decision-making processes and encouraging them to form attitudes and identify their values at this stage of their lives, was perceived by teachers to be a positive and effective means of ensuring that pupils would develop into empowered and participating citizens.

Perceptions of PSE

• Teachers' opinions and perceptions of PSE were varied. In secondary schools where PSE was an integral part of the timetable, PSE teachers themselves were in most cases enthusiastic and very positive in their assessment of the subject and the valuable benefits and opportunities it provided in promoting *"non-intellectual"* aspects of pupil development. Most secondary teachers acknowledged that the subject *"doubtlessly does some good"* while a few were less enthusiastic suggesting that it *"gives the less able ones hope of getting at least one GCSE"*.

• There was an impression conveyed by some grammar school teachers that PSE was a rather lightweight subject, with little intellectual value. Within the broader picture of academic achievement and accreditation the subject was perceived as *"not a lot of use"*. One or two treated the subject with some contempt, commenting that it was *"really a two-bit secondary subject"*. These views however did not reflect the majority of opinion. Most teachers (grammar and secondary) commented that while they knew little about the content of PSE, it made an important contribution to the school timetable in terms of *"whole child development"*.

• As with RE, teachers saw PSE as covering those *"social"*, *"sensitive"*, *"difficult"*, *"additional"*, *"controversial"* aspects of their subjects which some preferred to *"skim over"* or *"leave to the side"*. In this way, PSE was perceived as also *"filling the gaps"*. Significantly, teachers commented on a disparity between recent messages from the government for a more emphasis on personal, social and moral education and the reality in most schools that the formal programme of study for PSE is only afforded one or two periods a week on the timetable.

Conclusion

PSE teachers expressed a concern that PSE was not more readily recognised and accepted by teachers and senior managers in grammar and secondary schools. While they felt the subject had *"gained some ground"* there was still a long way to go. A teacher summarised her feelings by commenting,

> *I think it's rather sad and shortsighted that education in our society seems to be confined to the development of a fairly narrow knowledge base. We need to reconsider what our pupils really need once they leave the security and familiarity of the school.*

The Cross Curricular Themes

Throughout interviews, respondents were asked to consider where and how values featured through the Cross-Curricular Themes (CCTs) and, where appropriate, to identify how these impinged upon the various subjects which make up the formal curriculum. From teachers' responses, it became evident that several of the Cross-Curricular Themes were more prominent in their minds than others. Education for Mutual Understanding (EMU) was the most commonly mentioned CCT, followed by Cultural Heritage and Information Technology (though the latter was mentioned much less frequently). While most teachers were confident in providing evidence of how the themes permeate programmes of study, fewer teachers were able to provide concrete, practical examples of how the themes might actually be explored with pupils.

A concern regularly intimated by teachers, was that the introduction or inclusion of the cross-curricular themes in some areas of the curriculum is artificial and forced. Respondents commented that the implementation of the themes then became nothing more than a *"tick box exercise"* where teachers placed a "tick" against a theme each time it was featured in their teaching. These perceptions are corroborated in a recent cohort study of the Northern

Ireland Curriculum where teachers' dissatisfaction with the cross-curricular themes was focused very strongly on the "sense of artificiality which the CCTs were perceived to impose on the 'natural' content of individual subjects" (Harland et al, 1996:48).

Health Education

Teachers from a small range of subjects, namely HE, PE, PSE and Science, referred to opportunities for personal and social development through Health Education. Aspects of the PE programmes of study at all Key Stages were perceived to promote a positive self-image and self-confidence in pupils as part of their physical development. Teachers indicated how play in the early years encourages children to explore and experiment with movement and to develop a positive attitude towards physical activity. Older pupils are focused on increasing awareness of their physical capabilities and the physiological and social value of integrating regular exercise into their daily routines. Some of the topics featured in the Science, PSE and HE programmes of study relate directly to health issues, such as nutrition, hygiene and human development. Respondents reflected again on the formation of healthy and responsible attitudes in pupils towards these issues.

Social development was measured through the formation and management of healthy, social relationships with family, friends and others. Opportunities were perceived in all the subjects mentioned to further the development of positive social skills and attitudes. These were highlighted by the ability of pupils to work effectively with their peers, to form balanced judgements and to develop an understanding and acceptance of others.

Information Technology (IT)

The learning outcomes identified for this theme include,

> a knowledge and understanding of appropriate uses of IT, with a corresponding ability to apply it sensibly and with confidence... and a recognition of the effects which IT can and will have on themselves, other individuals, organisations and society. (NICC 1992)

Identifying values in this theme posed some problems for most teachers. Responses tended to focus on the permeation of technology through most aspects of life and the necessity for pupils to be familiar and comfortable with various tools of information technology. The computer was mentioned on many occasions and respondents highlighted the opportunities it provided for creative, communicative and educational activities along with various storage and labour saving benefits. Other perspectives concerned the impact of information technology on individuals and society and the responsibility which accompanied the widespread use of various IT tools.

A concern expressed by teachers was the increasingly technocratic nature of the curriculum and the perception of a potential shift away from human values and the value of the individual. One teacher commented that society tends to value what is beautiful and what is useful and suggested that an overemphasis on technology presents a distorted picture of what we consider to be of worth.

Economic Awareness

Economic Awareness aims,

> to develop in young people the ability to participate effectively as confident consumers, producers and citizens. (NICC 1992)

This theme was mentioned in connection with subjects under the Environment and Society area of study and on several occasions Mathematics. Teachers emphasised the value of pupils having a good working knowledge of this area in order to be able to make balanced and informed judgements and to discern what are appropriate actions in various situations. Teachers also commented on how pupils might be empowered to use relevant knowledge and to investigate issues which could have implications for the personal, social and economic welfare of individuals, communities and the wider society.

Careers Education

The concept of careers education is based on a belief that,

> individuals should be enabled to shape and direct the course of their lives as autonomous and responsible members of society, in order both to enhance the quality of personal life and contribution to the common good.
> (NICC 1992)

Several careers teachers were interviewed as part of the research and they commented quite extensively on the potential benefits of this cross-curricular theme in the personal development of pupils. Careers studies undertaken in the context of any subject were perceived to promote and enhance pupils' knowledge and understanding of themselves. Teachers indicated how, in considering further education or employment, pupils undertake a valuable *"inventory of their characteristics, skills and strengths"*. Opportunities are afforded pupils to identify and catalogue their personal qualities, strengths, interests, potential, abilities and values, *"to think essentially about who they are"*. Teachers felt that promoting self-awareness helped pupils to consider themselves in relation to their peers, friends, family and as members of society.

As well as gaining essential knowledge and skills though selected subjects, it was noted that pupils were also investigating appropriate personal skills and qualities and making important choices and decisions.

Teachers felt that self-awareness was promoted through all subjects to some degree, though English, HE, PSE, and RE appeared to offer more opportunities to pursue this objective. Teachers of English intimated how the use of language and the development of telephone and interview techniques also contribute to Careers Education. RE was perceived to offer opportunities for the development of self-awareness and to deal with issues related to lifestyle and ambition.

Many teachers felt they complemented the work of careers teachers by offering additional information relating to subjects and, where it was possible and appropriate, information regarding qualifications and career descriptions.

One issue raised by many teachers concerned pupils' transition from school to further education, employment and *"the wider world"*. A number of respondents referred to how the values upheld and transmitted within the school walls often contrasted markedly with those in institutions for further and higher education and in the workplace. Some teachers expressed concern that schools give little or no acknowledgement to this and offered only minimal preparation for the transition to the wider world.

One teacher commented,

> *It's a totally different ball game out there. Sometimes I think teachers and schools forget that. They communicate a set of values which are not always readily applicable or transferable to the bigger world of work and life.*

Education for Mutual Understanding (EMU) and Cultural Heritage

Respondents tended to address these two themes as one (under the term EMU), either because they recognised the two as being "conjoined" or because EMU was perceived to have incorporated Cultural Heritage. It became evident at an early stage during interviews that many teachers perceived EMU as being the quintessential expression of values within the curriculum. When discussing the values underpinning school life or specific subjects, respondents frequently mentioned EMU and many teachers' understanding of the concept of values seemed to stem from their knowledge and practice of this theme.

The objectives of EMU were referred to, in part or in their entirety, by a considerable number of respondents as they considered values in the curriculum. In articulating values perceived through activities and projects, teachers' responses were often informed by the objective which states that pupils should be enabled to,

> learn to respect and value themselves and others; to appreciate the interdependence of people within society; to know about and understand what is shared as well as what is different about their cultural traditions; and to appreciate how conflict may be handled in non-violent ways.
>
> (NICC 1990)

Teachers spoke of such experiences as:

> *helping pupils to gain a greater knowledge of themselves and others;*
>
> *developing less polarised views than their parents;*
>
> *improving teacher and school links with other schools and community;*
>
> *encouraging children to discover the truth about cultural traditions;*
>
> *helping pupils to discern what is important to them - what they value.*

When EMU was discussed as part of the formal curriculum, that is through the subject areas, teachers referred mainly to the Creative and Expressive subjects and English, History, HE, PSE and RE. Areas which were highlighted included interpersonal contact and associated issues, studies of personal, social and cultural identity and the positive effects of class discussions and debates. Several respondents made references to EMU being a focus for RE, as this was the *"moral conscience of the school"*. In response to this, many RE teachers said that they had *"backed off"* EMU activities and the *"EMU image"*, anxious that they would not become solely identified with the theme within the school. As indicated earlier some teachers were concerned that the inclusion of EMU in some areas was contrived and the links between topics and the theme at times tenuous. Some teachers also found it difficult to identify tangible links between the theme and their subject and a few said they *"just consider EMU if it happens incidentally"*.

EMU in practice

Since teachers identified EMU as a discernible values thread or as a few suggested, *"the present practice of values"* in the curriculum, it may be useful to briefly highlight what appeared to be the prevailing perceptions of the theme. Firstly, there was some considerable variation in the recognition and definition of the theme and a lack of cohesion in implementation in some schools. Most teachers appreciated that EMU goes beyond the generation of contact between Catholic and Protestant pupils, primarily through the Cross-Community Contact Scheme, though this was referred to by many. There were references made to European studies and opportunities for pupils to participate in projects and exchanges with their European counterparts. Several teachers also described EMU activities which had been undertaken by arranging visits and outings with elderly people and children with special needs, though the latter was a less common occurrence because of insurance issues, parental opinion and the logistics of arranging visits.

A small number of teachers referred to *"other colleagues"* who were *"doing 30 minutes of EMU a week"*, or who had dismissed it altogether, arguing that *"there just isn't time to worry about that as well"*. Some other teachers commented on the tendancy for schools to undertake detailed reviews of the inclusion of EMU throughout the curriculum, in order to fulfil the requirements of the DENI Inspectorate and then to *"shove these reports and implementation strategies in a drawer and forget about them"*. Teachers also commented on the crucial influence of senior management on the emphasis given to EMU and the success of the theme in the school. The personality and experience of a school's EMU co-ordinator and the level of support given to her by senior staff was also an important influence on the impact of EMU across the curriculum and through the school. One EMU co-ordinator commented,

EMU in our school is like Chinese Whispers. From the time of training to the drafting of a school policy to actual practice, EMU is often barely recognisable.

Some teachers commented that its aims and objectives gave EMU a strong identity and that for some schools this was *"out of kilter"*. On the other hand, one teacher commented that since the objectives so closely resembled the school's objectives, it was easy at times to *"let it all go by default"*. Others commented that they still did not feel confident handling the theme, that they felt they were being encouraged to *"sell"* something or that the requirements of the theme exceeded the remit of the teacher's role. The fact that EMU had been imposed through statutory orders still evoked some anger and resentment from a few teachers.

Most teachers expressed some degree of commitment to promoting and developing EMU in their subject area and school. Some indicated examples of where they felt teachers had failed to harness the full potential of EMU or as one teacher commented, *"missed the point"*. References were made to schools that initiated contact through the cross community contact scheme and had then not organised appropriate follow-up activities,

It's just not enough to load two sets of kids on a bus and let them do their own thing at the Icebowl. It takes a lot of planning and thinking.

A more detailed examination of teachers' perceptions of EMU and its introduction to the statutory curriculum in Northern Ireland is provided by a recent report (Smith and Robinson, 1996).

EMU as a 'ready-made' values dimension

Many of the teachers interviewed commented on the 'ready-made' nature of the values underpinning EMU and what they perceived to be widespread acceptance of these within the education system. Based on these perceptions of relevance and acceptability, a number of teachers demonstrated moderate to strong support for a values module or a values cross-curricular theme based on a range of aims and objectives similar to EMU. This support was accompanied by several positive and negative observations.

Firstly, it was suggested that by *"shaking out the values"* and adapting EMU, a new theme would be free of many of the negative connotations and suspicions surrounding EMU. Several respondents thought that the introduction of a values theme would shift teachers' thinking towards more universal concerns such as citizenship, social justice and human rights issues and offer more materials and guidance for exploring and discussing controversial issues. This would lead to an *"opening up"* and broadening out of the conceptual framework of EMU.

On the negative side, teachers warned that the introduction of *"something new or different"* would not be greeted enthusiastically by teachers who already felt over-burdened and under pressure. For this reason, a cross-curricular theme relating to values seemed more acceptable than a separate module or subject area. Some respondents felt there was an ambiguity associated with a theme relating explicitly to values and that teachers might face some difficulties attempting to *"tie down"* what on the surface would seem a rather nebulous concept. A few teachers also suggested that it was not entirely necessary to legislate for value dimensions in the curriculum, as values were already an integral part of teachers' daily practice and they simply did *"not have time to look for them"*. One individual commented, *"the good teacher is already doing it"*. Taking this a stage further, there was a concern that the inclusion and implementation of a values theme would be difficult to monitor and control, leaving teachers a free rein in their management and practice. Another comment expressed a concern regarding about articulating the intended outcomes of a values theme and the identification of suitable methods for assessing its impact and effects on pupils.

One issue about which teachers were almost unanimous in their responses, was the need for more appropriate pre- and in-service training for the delivery of EMU and any value-related themes. Many individuals expressed a desire for more opportunities to engage in personal development. They also pointed to a need for greater provision of guidance and materials so that they might be equipped with the confidence and knowledge to confront and explore affective and controversial issues.

EMU, as intimated earlier, was perceived by many teachers as a frame of reference for the values which currently underpin the curriculum. Many of them felt that the most profitable way to move forward was to build on the values and activities already in place from the permeation and implementation of EMU throughout the Northern Ireland Curriculum.

The relevance of the cross-curricular themes

The perception, by a number of teachers, that the cross-curricular themes were in some cases *"intrusive"*, *"confusing"*, *"additional"*, and *"extra"*, clearly suggested that they were not a priority or of significant importance to teachers. These comments were also indicative of a limited permeation of the themes throughout the curriculum. While many respondents did consider aspects of the themes important because *"they cover some areas which are outside of the timetabled subjects"*. Teachers in some subjects did not regard them as integral or essential components of a pupil's educational experience. In pursuing further explication of this perspective, teachers were asked what their aspirations were for each pupil leaving school, or at a more fundamental level, what they were aiming to produce.

Their responses in the first instance tended to centre around objectives which correlated with individual subjects. For example, one teacher stated that his objective was to *"equip pupils with scientific knowledge and methodical, investigative skills"*, and an English teacher's response was to *"empower pupils with effective language and communication skills"*. Teachers in other subject areas submitted similar knowledge or skills based objectives. When asked to consider what schools should be aiming to produce, the majority of responses focused first and foremost on the intellectual capabilities of pupils. *"An educated person"* or *"an intelligent, knowledgeable individual"* were two responses. Only a few individuals commented on the development of personal qualities or character of pupils.

These perceptions were further evidence of the apparent imbalance in the curriculum towards cognitive and knowledge based areas and dimensions. Teachers did not appear sufficiently convinced or motivated to spent further time on or give greater emphasis to the cross-curricular themes, when as they said themselves,

> *The emphasis is on other areas of the curriculum. We can't waste time with the themes. They're not what's important to headmasters, parents and pupils.*

Paralleled to these perspectives however, teachers expressed a willingness to promote and extend their delivery of the themes through their subject areas and beyond. This willingness was conditional however on a *"slackening"* in their workload and pressure, and on a changing emphasis in the Formal Curriculum.

Conclusions

A number of general conclusions may be drawn from teachers' perceptions of values in the Formal curriculum.

A compartmentalised perspective

Throughout the interviews, many teachers' perceptions of the Formal curriculum were presented from a subject oriented perspective. This approach was applied not only to their understanding of the curriculum, but also to perceptions of their own role in the school and the wider education system. Teachers repeatedly indicated, implicitly or explicitly, that they existed in a kind of "subject bubble" and that they engaged in relatively little collaborative contact with their colleagues to identify areas of overlap or commonality between subjects. In the Northern Ireland Cohort Study, teachers indicated that they "resisted links with other subjects" to avoid confusing pupils (Harland et al, 1996:61-62). Some individuals therefore admitted that they were aware of opportunities for potential overlap, but identified collaborative work as inappropriate, or expressed a lack of confidence or expertise in adopting this pedagogical approach. One or two teachers commented *"I have enough problems keeping abreast of my own subject area"*. Whitty, Rowe and Aggleton ratify these findings in their report on subjects and themes in the curriculum, when they comment,

> Most teachers do not have an understanding of what happens in other subject areas and indeed find it a considerable challenge to keep up with developments in their own subject. (Whitty, Rowe and Aggleton, 1994:26)

Findings in the Northern Ireland Curriculum Cohort Study also corroborate these points with references made to the "insularity of certain subject departments" and teachers explaining this in terms of "[defending] a subject's sense of identity" (p.52).

Other reasons submitted for the lack of collaboration include the perceived "stiffness" of a subject's own curriculum, the "time problem" and the constraints of "too many topics" in the curriculum (p.53). Research into pupils' perceptions of the curriculum reinforces the image of a "compartmentalised curriculum" and also points to pupils' inability to discern links because it's "not in the right boxes" (p.55).

Curriculum priorities

From teachers' responses and reviews of the curriculum, it was obvious that certain areas are prioritised. Teachers commented that timetabling and subject options offered to pupils clearly indicated in most cases, an emphasis on the core subjects of English, Maths and Science and a bias towards the accumulation of scientific and technological knowledge and skills. Many teachers identified without hesitation, areas which they felt were considered "valuable" by senior management, parents, DENI and the wider society. A large number of teachers engaged in Environment and Society, and Creative and Expressive areas of study complained that the increase in the proportion of time allocated to Science subjects imposed more limitations on their time and in some cases left teachers *"struggling to get through everything"*. Others commented on the narrow options which some pupils face in choosing subjects, having at some stage to decide between *"intellectual"*, cognitive subjects and creative, *"imaginative"* subjects. It was suggested that such a decisions are essentially a choice between *"academic"* subjects and what were widely regarded to be *"practical"*, *"expressive"*, *"minority"* or *"secondary"* subjects.

When these perceptions of the curriculum were examined in greater detail however, it emerged (at times more clearly than others), that individual schools' thinking and the nature of their values had some bearing on what was deemed important and what was prioritised. On some occasions these differences related to the type of school, (that is primary, secondary, grammar, integrated, special, controlled and maintained). At other times a school's own particular ethos and values appeared to have a strong influence on what was prioritised in the curriculum. As there were some limitations in gaining access to schools during the research, it is difficult to comment accurately or widely on this issue. Some indication of these priorities may be found however, under the Hidden Curriculum.

Finding the values dimension

Teachers did make a connection between creative and expressive subjects, PSE, HE and RE, and a values dimension in the curriculum. The perception and delivery of these subjects differed quite considerably in grammar and secondary schools.

Teachers in secondary schools suggested there was a greater emphasis on creative and expressive subjects and pinpointed examples of Drama and Art techniques being implemented throughout the curriculum subjects. They observed that affective-type strategies were *"strongly rejected by many grammar schools"* because they were regarded as *"secondary and second-rate"*. In contrast, secondary teachers regarded Drama in particular, with considerable enthusiasm, indicating its versatility and the opportunities it afforded less able and less outgoing pupils to participate in class.

In a similar vein, PSE and HE were also considered more important in many secondary schools, and treated with a degree of disdain by some grammar schools. Again, teachers in secondary schools identified value in these subjects, providing a *"point of contact for weaker students"* while also covering *"issues which are relevant and important to all pupils whatever their abilities"*. A few grammar school teachers acknowledged the value of PSE in a secondary school context, but criticised the apparently arbitrary structures governing the content and discussions in PSE and suggested it was *"hardly practical or useful in an academic environment"*, again reflecting a distinctive learning and curriculum emphasis. According to most teachers, RE seemed to have a notably higher status in most grammar and secondary schools.

Strengthening a values dimension within the formal curriculum

Teachers were generally supportive of the importance of a values dimension within the formal curriculum and constantly emphasised the importance of *"building into"* what already exists in the curriculum. As outlined earlier, many of the values inherent in EMU and Cultural Heritage were considered as an appropriate starting point, and the approaches employed and issues discussed in PSE, HE and RE give some guidance in ascertaining how a values dimension might be developed in practice. However teacher support was qualified by concerns that:

- the existing parameters for discourse in PSE, EMU and to a lesser extent RE were rather loose and indistinct, and that greater clarity and structure was required for a more widespread permeation of values and value-related discussions;

- the existing association of PSE and RE with values and moral education had already identified such issues as peripheral in many teachers' minds;

- lack of assessment or examination structures for the values dimension would confer in many minds a low status on the area;

- fuller integration of a values dimension into the formal curriculum would necessitate a change in or need for additional pedagogical techniques;

- addressing values in the curriculum would necessitate some knowledge of moral education and the philosophical debates surrounding this area, and this would raise significant questions about the capacity of teachers to take on the task.

Chapter five

Values and the informal curriculum

For the purposes of this chapter, the Informal Curriculum is defined as 'areas and aspects of school life located outside of the classroom'. Throughout this research, the term 'Informal Curriculum' pertained to a range of aspects and areas of school life including extra-curricular activities, school trips, pastoral care and discipline policies, and various domains of the school environment, such as the staffroom and playground. In this section elements of the Informal Curriculum will be considered in light of the values which were seen to underpin these areas of school life.

Extra-curricular activities

Teachers identified the potential for Music, Art and Drama to provide opportunities for pupils to express themselves through different mediums, respect and understand each other better, and generate a sense of *"cohesion, responsibility and even family"* in the school. They also drew attention to the public relations (PR) function of these subjects.

Teachers frequently commented, how Music, Drama, Media Studies, PE and Art were most valued once they had been, *"taken out of their subject pocket in the curriculum and transformed into plays, concerts and musical shows"*. All teachers in the Creative and Expressive area of study noted the changing emphasis and approach to Music and Drama when a school show or open day was approaching, commenting that *"senior management couldn't do enough to arrange teacher cover and access to the assembly hall"*. Music and Drama teachers made many references to the PR aspects of their subjects and even of their teaching roles when the school was seeking to *"sell itself"* to prospective parents and pupils, the Inspectorate or members of the community. Some mused over the fact that the very subjects which were projected as part of PR were those which received least emphasis and were apparently least valued during during school time.

School performance on the rugby field or hockey pitch was also recognised as an important factor in determining its status to the outside community.

Teachers spoke of the subtle and direct pressures they experienced from Head teachers to *"get a good result on Saturday"* and to ensure that the school projected a good image to its rivals. Teachers frequently referred to the dichotomy which existed in their attempts to accentuate a less competitive side to sports in the school and the demands to send a team onto a pitch against an opposing school team, *"out for the kill"*. Several school policies accommodated this by advocating the cultivation of an *"appropriate degree of competitiveness"*.

The pressure on schools to project a positive and successful image was perceived to require a concerted effort from teachers in the Creative and Expressive area, though there was some concern that this could prove detrimental to the preparation and delivery of the programmes of study. On a visit to a probationary music teacher, a Board advisor related how she discovered the teacher was experiencing problems finding time to plan and actually teach lessons, because she was spending so much time with the school choir and orchestra rehearsing for the school prize distribution, Open day and Christmas concert. Other teachers with several years of experience commented that they also experienced problems at certain times of the year, *"trying to get everything done"*.

The status of Creative and Expressive subjects was not improved by their assignation to the *extra*-curricular dimension in some schools. Teachers commented that this simply confirmed in the minds of some senior teachers and departments, that these presented pupils with opportunities *"to relax"* or at best to develop some *"leisure skills"*. A few language teachers felt that French, Spanish and German were also part of the *"leisure skills"* group.

The type of sport played in schools was perceived by some teachers to carry particular values. Some controlled and voluntary grammars were defined as the 'rugby' schools and 'traditional' schools which were *"still clinging to the old ethos of developing brilliance"*. Such schools were also perceived as being very competitive, and in some cases "Victorian", in their emphasis on rugby, hockey, rowing and cross-country and some were still seen to be contemptuous of soccer, basketball and some leisure centre activities. Several teachers suggested these were *"more suitable"* for secondary schools. Sports such as Gaelic football, hurley and camogie were in most instances, strongly associated with maintained schools, though some teachers noted that a few maintained grammar schools are engaging in *"the rugby culture"*. Several teachers commented that it was difficult to *"throw off the political, religious and even sectarian badges"* on these sports.

In positive terms, extra-curricular activities were seen to present opportunities for collaboration between departments and individual teachers. Respondents commented on how staff relations and collegiality improved remarkably during preparations for a school play or show, and how once established, links and partnerships had the potential to generate more cross-curricular projects. As one teacher remarked,

Once you get to work with some of the others, you find they're actually alright ... there are also some other opportunities to work together.

Educational visits and field trips

School field trips, outings and educational visits are organised for a variety of purposes. Teachers provided examples where these arose through EMU projects, Music, the Arts, Geography and environmental projects. Trips such as these were recognised as educationally and socially valuable by the majority of teachers. Geography, Music and History teachers commented that taking children out of school and *"into the world outside"* made certain issues *"come alive"* in a way which was not possible within the classroom. Studies of the environment were particularly difficult to recreate in class and teachers commented that there was no substitute for the real experience of the seashore, peatland or forest. Several primary teachers related how educational visits are particularly beneficial to children from deprived backgrounds who were otherwise not likely to gain such experiences.

Despite the positive experiences and outcomes associated with school trips, teachers frequently mentioned the difficulties and complexities of arranging even an afternoon away from school. Taking a group of pupils out of school requires transport, additional teacher assistance, teacher cover (in post-primary schools), insurance, parental permission, funding, assuming extra responsibility, extra supervision and, according to all teachers, *"energy"*. Many respondents said that they had been discouraged from organising trips and visits because of the *"hassle"* and *"extra work"* and sometimes because of a *"lack of support"* from other staff members. Attempts to undertake visits to special schools and neighbouring schools as part of EMU had sometimes been hindered by the need for extra assistance, parental concern and the cost of insurance. One teacher summarised the general feeling of teachers,

You know it's all worth it when you get them out there, but the hassle of it all does put you off a bit.

School assemblies

Some attention was given to the format and purpose of school assemblies. Teachers in many schools felt there had been perceptible changes in the content and scheduling of assemblies. Some schools had reduced the number of whole school assemblies and in several cases restricted them to a series of announcements, omitting any type of *"worship"*. The head teacher and his or her religious views were considered to strongly influence the structure and delivery of assemblies. Most teachers discussed the relevance and value of holding assembly, and the nature of the messages which they felt were conveyed. Most teachers agreed that a weekly or bi-weekly assembly with a reading or prayer and hymn was acceptable. Some thought the whole concept of school worship was *"rather outdated"* and the practice of 'imposed' worship *"ethically incorrect"*. A few RE teachers in controlled post-primary schools felt it was less than adequate and that the worship element was not always approached in *"an appropriate manner"*. Other RE teachers felt it was a valuable opportunity for pupils who might otherwise never experience church worship to be exposed to some form of collective worship. Whatever their religious outlook, however teachers felt it provided a valuable opportunity to bring the whole school together and to promote some degree of cohesion and a sense of group identity.

School policies

A review of school policies provided an important insight into the values that schools professed and as an indicator of what was considered to be 'valuable' by the school as an institution.

School policies were a major topic for discussion, particularly with senior management and head teachers. During the course of the fieldwork many schools were in the process of completing pastoral care policies, discipline policies and school statements regarding behaviour, ethos, school rules and homework. Policies stated a broad and diverse range of aims and objectives, too numerous to list. These related to the promotion and development of the pupils' physical, personal, inter-personal, moral, social, emotional, spiritual, mental, intellectual, aesthetic and cultural well-being. The language of policy statements laid great emphasis on "encouraging", "facilitating", "developing", "respecting", "considering", "supporting", "celebrating" and "valuing" the individuals, relationships, processes, methods, structures and environments within the school.

When asked to comment on pastoral care or discipline within a school, senior managers on many occasions quoted or read substantial extracts from their policies, commenting with some pride on the amount of effort and time given to discussing and formulating these policies. Other teachers indicated that whole staff consultation was not as widespread as might have been suggested, and that in many cases senior management, year heads or tutors, draft a policy on which staff are then invited to comment. Some teachers admitted they were reluctant to offer comments (especially in larger schools) as *"you can come across as a bit of a troublemaker if you say too much"* and *"if it's got as far as the teachers, there's not much chance of changing anything"*. These attitudes gave the impression that in some schools, policies are imposed on teachers rather than developed through discussion and collaboration. Several head teachers commented on the importance of *"bringing the staff along with you"*, but were less forthcoming in explaining how this was achieved in practice. Whatever approach is adopted in drafting a school policy, there appeared to be considerable consensus that, *"the aims are attainable only through the full, unbroken co-operation of parents, pupils and teachers"*.

Pastoral care

The pervasive nature of pastoral care was highlighted in many discussions with head teachers and other senior managers. The provision of a framework which promotes social, emotional and moral development was widely acknowledged as an important and indeed essential part of the school's role.

Pastoral care policies set out a range of strategies and objectives relating to the well-being of the *"whole child"*. Common to many of these policies was the development of the *"full potential of each child"*, a commitment to helping each child to acquire self-discipline and a sense of responsibility and the development of each child's awareness of herself, others and her environment. Some policies focused on specific values, outlining aims to *"instil respect for the religious and moral values of the different cultures in our society"* and to *"understand another's viewpoint and the principles, beliefs and values which underlie it"*.

A few schools had adopted a mechanism for considering pastoral care and the *"whole child"* focusing on various parts of the whole self, namely the bodily self, sexual self, social self, vocational self and moral self. Teachers felt that this approach facilitated a more in-depth and individualised approach to the consideration of pupils pastoral care and development.

Many members of senior management suggested that the values promoted by teachers through pastoral care had not radically changed over the years. They still shared a concern for the individual child, for their personal and social development and an ability to progress, achieve, communicate and integrate with others. What senior management and teachers themselves felt had changed was the growing expectation that teachers would deal with and assume responsibility for an ever-expanding range of pastoral issues.

Many teachers felt there were difficulties in obtaining a widely acceptable and workable definition of pastoral care. Teachers spoke of the problems surrounding the identification and implementation of a suitable approach and the need to achieve consensus and consistency.

While many schools had a well-defined structure and procedure for pastoral care administered by specific members of staff, such as year heads and pastoral tutors, a great number of teachers still expressed some concern and anxiety about their own roles in this area. A range of issues were raised in relation to this, including:

- a concern over the growing number of increasingly serious issues associated with contemporary 20th century living which were brought into the school and classroom, e.g. drugs, violence, physical and sexual abuse;

- a feeling that parents and wider society are content to *"offload"* such problems and associated issues along with the accompanying stresses onto teachers;

- considerable anxiety over teachers lack of confidence and training to handle these and other similar issues;

- a concern that teachers may have to clarify and defend their own attitudes, beliefs and values, many of which they feared may be quite contrary to those of their pupils;

- a fear of the pressures of responsibility and accountability to parents, school and society in general;

- discomfort with the expanding nature of the non-teaching role.

Discipline in schools

In a large number of schools, pastoral care and discipline policies were formulated together to reflect the view that each has implications for the other. Teachers suggested that, for example, behavioural problems often originated from a problem with learning in the classroom or problems related to a situation at home. Several head teachers explained that pastoral care and discipline "*go hand in hand*".

Discipline systems were clearly an important institution in schools and senior managers frequently commented that it was imperative for teachers and pupils to fully understand and recognise the framework and boundaries of the school discipline system. Equally important was the teachers' commitment to, and consistency in imposing sanctions for a variety of misdemeanours. In a number of policies, misbehaviour and offences had been categorised into degrees of minor, serious and gross misconduct. These ranged from talking in class to various types of "*horseplay*" to physical assault on a pupil or member of staff. Within the comparatively small number of policies reviewed, there was a strong consensus in the definitions of what constituted these various degrees of indiscipline. However, in conversations with individual teachers, what constituted a minor or serious offence was not always so readily definable.

A number of responses revealed a reluctance or disinterest in the application of discipline policy. A number of teachers admitted that it "*is very tedious telling the same fellow off for the same thing over and over*", so they had "*just ignored him or given up*". Others argued that there was little point in referring discipline matters to a more senior member of staff as "*they can't be bothered*", "*won't do anything anyway*" or are "*too busy with paperwork*".

Some teachers made brief reference to the procedures established in their discipline policies for dealing with "*that small trouble-making minority*". Most revealed that permanent removal or expulsion was comparatively rare and also difficult to instigate. One secondary school teacher stated,

> *You can't get rid of them now. You're stuck with them. The policy now is to help them deal with things in school. Well, you're wasting your time if you ask me....boys like that never change.*

Teachers debated the advantages and disadvantages of suspending pupils, isolation from their peers and removal from the classroom. The majority felt that a brief period of suspension could be beneficial, allowing time for an unpleasant incident to be dealt with or for a volatile situation to settle down. Teachers also referred to school policies for reintegrating a pupil and the continuing surveillance of potentially explosive situations. Suspension was perceived as giving a pupil time and space to consider his actions and to renegotiate his place in the school community. Some teachers commented that it was also the *"only way to get the parents involved"*, and to embark on a home-school strategy for dealing with a pupil. Most teachers commented that in their schools, removal from a classroom was emphasised as a last resort and in a few it was not an option at all. While they felt it was important to provide support for the offender, they did argue there were situations and pupils for whom removal from the class or school was the most effective or indeed the only possible course of action.

Many teachers made reference to probationary teachers and their *"overconcern"* with discipline issues. Probationary teachers themselves admitted anxieties about *"establishing themselves"* and managing to *"keep things under control"*. In order to promote the idea of partnership in discipline between teachers and pupils, contracts had been introduced in some schools. When new pupils enrol at these schools they are asked to sign a contract of agreement which states their understanding of, and agreement to respect and obey school rules. Teachers felt this was a *"mature and adult way of securing some commitment and order"*. Teachers commented that the partnership approach also relied heavily on parents and their commitment to the school's discipline policy. They gave a variety of examples where parents had been involved successfully in resolving a pupil's behavioural and attitudinal problems. The implementation of various approaches (report cards, letters from principals, home and school visits and school tribunals) had all been explored as possible approaches.

Teachers stated that despite guidelines established by the school regarding inappropriate and unacceptable behaviour discipline was ostensibly *"down to the individual"*. Punative approaches were still the most common response to indiscipline. Many spoke of developing their own sanctions in the classroom, in some cases, *"regardless of what goes on in the rest of the school"*. Others commented on the leniency of their school discipline code, complaining that,

> *No matter what they say or do, you can't isolate them or remove them from the class. It's just not realistic and they know your hands are tied. Some of them play on it.*

Statements of school values

A number of statements of school aims were examined. These revealed a considerable degree concerning their commitment to the promotion of:

- responsible, considerate behaviour
- a disciplined and caring atmosphere
- willingness and co-operation
- a sense of belonging and loyalty
- the pursuit of academic excellence balanced by an appreciation of leisure.

In Special schools, pupils were expected as far as was possible to abide by a defined set of school rules. One teacher outlined that pupils were expected to,

- obey simple rules
- develop a sense of responsibility and truthfulness
- make simple choices
- have respect for others and property
- learn to share
- assume personal responsibility for actions.

Most of the policies examined were based on broadly Christian principles, though some (particularly maintained schools) made this commitment more explicit in their aims, for example statements that the school is concerned with,

- above all, deepening Christian faith and affirming its practice;
- bringing each young person closer to God;
- advocating a powerful and benign corporate life in which values and attitudes concerning relationships between individuals and groups are lived out and not merely advocated ('Towards a whole school policy for Catholic Schools', CCMS);
- the development of a strong sense of community and an atmosphere enlivened by the Gospel values of freedom and charity (Gravissimum Educationis, The Vatican Council, p.34).

Integrated schools often place a strong emphasis on community both within and outside the school. There was also an emphasis on whole child development. Because all of the integrated schools in Northern Ireland were established fairly recently, teachers spoke of a need for a high degree of co-operation between staff, pupils and parents, in order to make progress. Some of the aims identified by integrated schools included,

- to provide a happy, caring school;
- to remember that children come first; and
- to hope, work, and pray for greater social harmony in Northern Ireland.

Special school policies placed considerable emphasis on the affirmation and value of all pupils and their respective strengths and weaknesses. Respect and understanding were considered paramount to the development of a positive atmosphere and thriving school environment. They also drew attention to the importance of encouraging pupils to attempt new activities, *"to have a go"* and in doing so, to develop accurate perceptions of their abilities and realistic expectations for their futures. Teachers made reference to the vital links and partnerships between teaching staff, therapists, parents, transport drivers and social services in securing the provision of adequate and appropriate care and education for the pupils.

Homework policies were built into many school policies, giving clear guidelines to pupils and parents of the objectives of the policy and the expectations of the school regarding pupils' homework. Teachers outlined their perceptions of the value of homework, suggesting that homework,

- encourages pupils to establish a quiet place to study;
- provides opportunities for parents to be involved in a child's progress;
- carries on the learning process at home;
- allows pupils to consolidate class work;
- helps pupils to establish self-discipline in their study.

Many of the school policies which were examined, focused on the *"totality of the learning experiences"* and *"whole child development"*. While many teachers pledged their support of these aims, they admitted that there was often a considerable gulf between the rhetoric of the policies and the realisation of this in the day to day running of the school. Teachers explained that they experienced difficulties *"making it all concrete"*, and *"turning the theory of school policies into practice"*. A few teachers also thought that those who drafted the policies were removed from daily classroom practice,

> *Part of the problem is that the developers of this policy sit up there in their Ivory tower and the reality down here is actually a bit different.*

The physical environment of the school

Teachers' and pupils' perceptions of various aspects of the physical environment of the school were considered to be *"values indicators"* by many respondents. They described a number of locations in their school in terms of the messages which they communicated about the overall values and image of the school.

Teachers commented on the internal and external environment, the use of colour, light, space and texture throughout their schools and the potential effects of these on teaching and learning experiences. The general state of repair of classrooms (including decor, furniture and light) was a significant contributory factor to the extent of many teachers' contentment, motivation and commitment,

> *It definitely has an effect on my motivation. Sometimes more than others. There are days when I just can't face that room, its so dark and drab.*

Some others said that they hardly noticed or thought about the state of their classrooms, but when asked to consider them, some remarked that they were *"not very inspiring"*, *"they could do with a lick of paint"*, and *"my classroom walls just contribute to the whole feeling of imprisonment"*.

• Classrooms

Primary school classrooms were portrayed as much more likely to be bright and colourful, decorated in many cases with displays of children's work. Several teachers drew a distinction between primary and post-primary classrooms, commenting on the lack of colour in many post-primary classrooms and comparatively fewer classroom displays of pupils' work. Discussions centred around the positive and negative effects of displaying pupils' work and this issue is also explored as part of the Hidden Curriculum in the next chapter.

Teachers in Special schools underlined the importance of a colourful, interesting and stimulating environment especially for children with very severe learning difficulties. The provision and use of space, textures, light and colour were perceived as an integral part of the learning and development process, though teachers also acknowledged the positive and stimulating effects it had on their own teaching. Sensory gardens and outdoor activities were also described as providing important stimulation.

- The staffroom

  The staffroom was described in various ways, from a *"haven of peace"* to a corner of *"disharmony and disinterest"*. Staffrooms clearly serve different purposes in different schools. Some teachers saw it as a place for respite and for *"recharging the batteries"*, a friendly, relaxed, supportive and comfortable space, which in some schools was implicitly understood as "out of bounds" to the Head teacher and/or senior management. In other schools the atmosphere was unfriendly, uncommunicative and uncomfortable and teachers commented that they sought out *"other lunchtime options or company"*. Some staffrooms were used more as preparation and "marking" rooms and others were located so far from teachers' classrooms that *"it takes half of lunchtime getting there!"* The sort of reception which visitors to the staffroom receive was also perceived to be an indicator of the values and atmosphere which pertain to the school.

- Reception areas

  Teachers often commented on the impressions which entrance areas and the school reception convey to visitors. The provision of a seating area, displays of pupils' work, clearly placed signs and directions and the type of atmosphere experienced on arrival were all perceived to be indicative of image and school values. Several teachers thought that this reflected the head teachers' values more accurately, as in their schools, s/he was usually instrumental in making the decisions regarding this environment.

- The playground

  Teachers were asked to comment on the physical layout of playgrounds and the use of these spaces. A large number of teachers admitted they had not given the matter much consideration while others strongly advocated changes in play area arrangements or felt that the present playgrounds were adequate and that any improvements *"would only attract vandals"*. A few teachers mentioned that their schools had undertaken environmental projects which had included pupil participation in the redesign of their playground. They explained how time spent in the playground was valuable in providing opportunities for play, games, interaction and teamwork, and these schools felt that pupils should be proud of their playground and *"claim some ownership of it"*. Grassy areas and gardens had also been planned in some schools by pupils. Other teachers pointed out however, that pupils were often then prohibited from using 'green areas'. One teacher commented how pupils in her school had carefully designed and planted a small flower garden, but that on completion, the garden was declared 'out of bounds'.

Many teachers, particularly in post-primary schools, were fairly unaware of what occurred in the playground, beyond football or other games. A few commented that *"that's the best way...what happens out there should stay out there"*. There was a sense in which the playground was 'out of bounds' for teachers, that it was the *"children's domain"*. The playground was also perceived to be responsibility of lunchtime supervisors. Several primary schools were undertaking planned lunchtime activities of games and "environmental play" and others had drawn up a booking sheet for playground games, *"so that the boys and their football don't take over"*.

• The library

Teachers reported a decline in the use of school libraries for reading purposes and a diminishing interest amongst pupils in reading. A considerable number of post-primary teachers indicated that the school library had been *"absorbed into an English teacher's classroom"*, or *"shoved into a storeroom"*. The school library was also reported to serve a variety of purposes including, use as an additional classroom, a sixth form study, a teachers' marking room, a video and television room and a musical instrument store. In many cases use of the library for reading purposes was an uncommon activity. Teachers recognised that such anomalous use of school libraries communicated implicit messages to pupils such as the value placed on reading and the use of books in relation to computers and the establishment of Information Technology suites. Comments were also made about the lack of emphasis on independent reading and the demise of reading for pleasure as the immediacy and accessibility to computer software increases.

Conclusion

Teachers expressed genuine surprise at the abundance of opportunities within the informal curriculum for the transmission and discussion of values. Clearly, the provision and content of pastoral care policies and school value statements were perceived as potentially the most explicit communications of a school's values. However, teachers were also quick to recognise that the practices underpinning such policies do not always reflect the original intentions. The nature of the physical environment of the school was also seen to transmit sometimes quite subtle messages about values.

Chapter six

Values and the hidden curriculum

The hidden curriculum is generally perceived to be a rather nebulous concept. Meighan (1981) defines it as "all the other things that are learnt during schooling in addition to the official curriculum" (p.52). Bottery (1990) describes it in a variety of ways. He suggests that the hidden curriculum may be covert and used to "manipulate the unwary" or as that which "goes on in schools...and is seen as the manner in which the formal curriculum is conducted". The hidden curriculum may also be regarded as largely unintended, consisting of activities and policies which are "practiced in an unthinking way" involving "activities whose effect...was never recognised in the first place" (p.97). For the purposes of this research teachers were not provided with these explicit definitions, but their responses often referred to various aspects of school life which involved *"hidden agendas"*, *"covert actions"* and *"unspoken arrangements and policies"*.

Questions relating to school ethos or climate were presented to teachers as a means of focusing discussions about values underpinning the hidden curriculum. The term 'ethos' was widely recognised and used by many teachers. Some regarded it as an *"in word"* or *"buzz word"* and this was reflected in the many references which were made to its inclusion in school policies. An effective working definition of ethos is provided by the SCCC (as part of a conference on school climate and ethos) is "the outward expression of the norms, beliefs and values reflecting consensus and conflict in schools" (SCCC 1994:1).

Teachers were asked to comment on the many factors which influence and affect 'ethos' and this led to the identification and subsequent discussion of an eclectic range of issues and activities. These included the organisation and delivery of the curriculum, timetabling, management styles, decision-making processes, opportunities for staff development, discipline and classroom management. (Some of these areas have already been addressed through the formal and informal curriculae). It also emerged quite strongly from interviews, that at the heart of school ethos lies a complex web of inter-personal relationships between teachers, pupils and parents.

This chapter will briefly outline the main observations made by teachers. To begin, the first section examines general perceptions and definitions of ethos. Following this is a review of various school structures and policies and the 'hidden' values which were seen to underpin these. Teachers' perceptions of the tri-partite relationship between teachers, pupils and parents is then explored, followed by a brief study of the school's relationship with the wider community.

Defining 'ethos'

Teachers agreed that ethos is a relatively difficult concept to describe or define accurately. There was a strong feeling that each school would evolve its own unique definition appropriate to its own particular circumstances. Some individuals referred to ethos as *"the development of community"* or a *"community feeling"*. Others talked about *"whole school loyalty"*, *"the identification and pursuit of common goals"*, *"morale"* and *"positive relationships"*. The concept of community and a sense of belonging were common themes in many responses. Teachers identified the positive effects on pupils (and themselves) of feeling part of a school community. It was made evident by teachers that truly "belonging", meant participating fully in the school community and being accepted, respected and valued by the other members. One teacher described ethos as *"the sum of all the parts"*, but emphasised how this was more than just a collection of individuals; that the nature of interaction and relationships existing between the parts culminated in the creation of *"an underlying culture"*. Some teachers gave a general description of the ethos in their schools through a variety of comments,

> *Ours is fairly much academic and ambition-oriented.*

> *The school has cultivated a caring and accepting atmosphere.*

> *Ours is positive, industrious and friendly.*

> *I would say there's a big emphasis on achievement and competition.*

> *Focusing staff and pupils to look beyond the academic side and consider recreation, values and general knowledge.*

It was notable that head teachers and senior management gave the most positive responses whilst many teachers concentrated on more negative aspects of ethos.

Many teachers also made references to a "Christian ethos" and in maintained schools teachers spoke of a "Catholic ethos". The latter has been defined as "...an atmosphere enlivened by the Gospel values of freedom and charity" (Gravissimum Educationis 1966). Head teachers referred to school ethos being *"Christ-centred"* and *"created by making explicit in school what is implicit in the Gospel"*. In practical terms, this was articulated through policies of equality and respect for all pupils irrespective of their abilities, the pursuit of excellence and the achievement of potential for each pupil. There was also a strong emphasis on pastoral care and the spiritual growth of pupils. However, it became easier to discern the values underlying school ethos when teachers described the structural arrangements and relationships within their own schools.

The organisation of learning

A number of structural arrangements for the organisation of learning were identified as reflecting values underpinning school life. Some of these have already been mentioned in the earlier chapters on the formal curriculum and informal curriculum.

Emphases within the curriculum

Teachers frequently commented on the particular emphases which their school placed on different aspects of the curriculum. Most concluded that science and technology subjects receive greater attention and are promoted as more *"valuable subjects"*. Teachers felt that this was fairly obvious to pupils, not least, because of the amount of time allocated to these subjects in the timetable. In the Northern Ireland Curriculum Cohort Study, the appropriacy and relevance of subjects as perceived by pupils was seen to be influenced "by the values inherent in the school timetable" and as one teacher commented, this included the amount of time given to a subject (Harland et al, 1996:180).

Several teachers commented that the compartmentalised structure of the curriculum gave pupils the impression of a *"disjointed and segmented learning process"*. It was argued that this might encourage pupils to become selective by only engaging with parts of the curriculum which were perceived to be valuable and ignoring the remainder. Some teachers felt that subject disciplines should be promoted *"only as a vehicle for learning"* and that they should not *"blind pupils to the greater picture"* of a broad and rich learning experience.

The Transfer Procedure

An aspect of the education system in Northern Ireland which was raised in conversations with conspicuous regularity was the Transfer Procedure (commonly referred to as the 'Eleven Plus'). Primary teachers (and some post-primary) were most animated in their discourse, detailing various school procedures and narrating anecdotal experiences of the selection process. The approach adopted to this examination was perceived by teachers to be a *"good indicator of the education system's values"* or a *"tell-tale sign of a school's values"*.

The majority of teachers mentioned some change in the curriculum which was delivered to pupils in P5 and P6 attributed to the transfer tests,

> *You find the creative and expressive subjects dropping out.*

> *Well, there isn't much time for geography. You're too busy getting their science up to scratch. Some areas disappear altogether.*

Teachers stressed the pressure placed upon teachers and pupils in the year approaching the 'Eleven plus' and the accompanying shift in the content and teaching strategies in many schools. Several respondents referred to primary schools where *"streaming"* occurred as early as P3,

> *Streaming is not done formally, but teachers know at that stage who to concentrate on and who really hasn't a chance.*

When this phenomenon was queried with other teachers they demonstrated little surprise, usually going on to recount other similar situations.

Teachers also spoke of the pressure on pupils to perform well and to gain a grammar school place. They referred to the extra work, special tuition and Saturday morning classes offered by schools and often demanded by parents, and the promise of rewards from parents,

> *It's not unusual for the parents to make promises of holidays on the continent, or some big present if they pass.*

> *Oh, a reward is standard procedure you know, a bike at 'Eleven plus' and a car at 'A' level.*

Teachers frequently spoke of the pressures experienced by children with considerable concern, commenting that in some cases, children were *"just put through too much"* and parents often *"resort to bribery when they realise their expectations are too high"*.

Respondents also spoke of the pressure exerted by head teachers and parents on the P6 and P7 teachers *"to get as many through as possible"* with high grades. A number of teachers commented that their head teachers had approached them and indicated that he *"expected the same excellent results as last year"*. This expectation, according to teachers was proffered without any consideration of the present P7's abilities, *"I'm expected to perform miracles up here"*.

Many of the teachers interviewed suggested there is an unreasonable amount of pressure surrounding the Transfer Procedure and stated that they were strongly opposed to the intensive preparation undertaken in many schools and to the procedure itself. However they also expressed a sense of being *"trapped"* and caught up in the system and commented that there was little they could do, except to provide as much support as possible for their pupils. In primary schools (mostly in rural areas) where many children had opted out of the transfer procedure, Board advisors referred to the *"striking contrast"* in the curriculum followed and the climate pervading the upper school.

Many secondary teachers were critical of the effects of the transfer procedure, commenting that they had to cope with the short-term and long-term effects of failure on children and *"to try to undo the damage"*. Others accused the transfer system of *"setting children up to lose"*, suggesting that prior to the tests, most teachers could judge quite accurately how well different pupils would perform and *"identify those likely to fail"*.

Primary school teachers also pointed out that as well as making the potentially traumatic transition from primary to post-primary school, pupils discovered that only negligible references were made to their primary studies or experiences. One teacher commented that, *"there is little sense of continuity, and it's just like starting from scratch"*. Another said, *"It seems that when you start the 'big school', you should forget all about primary - it's for babies"*. This seemed to suggest, that once children reached grammar or secondary school, what had gone before in primary school was to a large extent forgotten and was not perceived as "valuable", at least not in any explicit manner.

'Streaming' pupils

The practice of 'streaming' pupils according to their abilities was discussed with many post-primary teachers. They identified a range of issues relating to teachers' attitudes to lower stream pupils and their restricted access to some aspects of the curriculum. While teachers were reluctant to criticise colleagues, they did indicate that it was not unusual for lower ability pupils to be seated at the back of the classroom, for teachers to *"skip over more difficult bits"* and *"not to chase up"* their homework. The *"cabbage class"* as one teacher said they were known in some schools *"slips to the bottom of the heap and pupils find they are all but ignored"*.

Since behavioural problems were frequently associated with lower ability pupils, several teachers said that these children are often ostracised by the system. The system, as one teacher argued, contains a well-defined but covert set of values where pupils are expected,

> *to be well-behaved all of the time, to speak only when spoken to in class, fit every attainment target and to originate from a good middle-class background with parents who only come to school on open nights.*

Teachers who had worked with pupils with learning and behaviour difficulties were sometimes encouraged by senior management with comments such as,

> *as long as they're not harming the furniture or themselves, you're doing a good job.*

It was suggested by a few teachers that the removal of pupils from the form class to a 'remedial class' was considered to be legitmate even when the problem was one of behaviour rather than learning. It was also suggested that pastoral care policies did not always provide a framework for responding to learning difficulties and it was acceptable for teachers to strongly impose their own expectations and values on pupils.

The school as 'a business'

Teachers highlighted the strength of the image of the "school as a business". Respondents referred to the *"depersonalising"* effect of concepts drawn from the business world, concepts concerned with marketability, accountability, the management of budgets, and input and output judged by GCSE, 'A' level results and the percentage of university entrants.

References were also made to the hierarchical system in schools and the prominence of a vertical structure. Teachers commented how *"everything moves up"* in the school system. Pupils progress *"up through the school"* and teachers move up the salary scale or promotion ladder. Teachers also spoke of teaching strategies which are based on *"top down"* approaches, pitching lessons at more able pupils and considering those on the lower rungs of the ability ladder afterwards. In this type of structure, there is less opportunity for adopting a horizontal perspective of the curriculum or promoting development across the curriculum. Teachers felt that this made it much more difficult to gauge pupils' experiences of the curriculum or to *"keep a check on what is going in"* at any one time. The value of the holistic learning experience for a pupil at any one stage in their school career was therefore, according to teachers something of *"an unknown quantity"*.

The teacher-pupil relationship

The nature of the exchange between teachers and pupils was perceived to be one of the main interactions through which values are defined and communicated.

Respondents were asked to consider the principles and attitudes which they adopted in the process of teaching and learning. Many teachers asserted that there are clear lines of demarcation between the two processes with the implication of a one-way process where teachers teach and pupils learn. A few teachers did feel that the processes were actually one and that teachers and pupils were *"on the same road"*, however this was a minority view. One teacher commented,

> *You've got to let them know that you're in charge. I don't think you can drop that for a second. Therefore when I teach, I'm in control. If I say I'm a learner, who's in control then?*

Defining the 'good' teacher

Most teachers recognised the notion of the 'good' teacher but found this difficult to define with any accuracy. Teachers commented that the production of good exam results was one important indicator, though it was still difficult to ascertain exactly how well pupils had been taught. Several teachers pointed out that a 'good' teacher might well have been *"teaching practically the same syllabus the same way for the last 19 or 20 years"* with no variation in technique, resources or classroom management. They also talked referred to the inspirational teacher, "who has something startling and memorable to say, and...could illuminate ...an aspect of life" (Lynch 1995:72). Several teachers felt that the pressures imposed by the curriculum and by senior staff in schools had eradicated *"the light and spark that makes some teachers different"*. Teachers were unanimous in their agreement that it is not possible to teach without *"giving something of themselves"*, although it was somewhat difficult to discern what exactly this meant in practice.

Primary teachers, in particular spoke of the value of delegating minor responsibilities to pupils in their class. A class monitor or helper system was perceived as an important means of involving pupils and sharing the responsibility for the tidiness and organisation of the classroom and for supporting the teacher by distributing books or running errands. Special school teachers drew attention to this role, commenting on the positive effects it had on children's self-confidence and sense of responsibilty. These teachers also adopted a much more explicit approach to the affirmation of pupils and spoke of encouraging collective praise from other class members. Pupils were made to *"feel good and feel valued"* in their contributions, no matter how small. They were also made more aware of each others' strengths and areas of need and encouraged to develop a greater sense of empathy, understanding and community.

Several teachers commented that a 'good' teacher might be recognised by the ability to meet the needs of all pupils, especially those who were perceived as "less able." One aspect of teaching which cropped up frequently in interviews, was the teaching methods adopted in teaching lower ability pupils. Several respondents revealed that schools dissuaded the "low achiever" from choosing some options in the curriculum, if they felt it would interfere with the progress of the *"more able pupils"*. One teacher also intimated that,

> *There are times when teachers can't be bothered with the hassle and extra work with a less able kid. They just get them to choose something else.*

Teachers regularly complained about the dearth of suitable materials for their lower ability students. The Northern Ireland Curriculum Cohort study also highlighted this point, commenting that, *teachers often had to compile extra resources of their own and were unable to give less able pupils the extra attention they needed.*

(Harland et al, 1996:179)

Some teachers, mostly in the secondary context commented on the *"crucial differences"* that appropriate learning and teaching strategies could make to pupils' progress. They referred to the rewards of "child-centred learning" and "pupil-oriented learning", both of which focus on the individual needs and abilities of pupils. Such an approach, noted teachers, clearly communicated the value of the individual pupil and enhanced their self-esteem and self-confidence. Several respondents felt that teaching in secondary schools required more creativity and imagination on the part of the teacher, in order to facilitate greater access to the curriculum for lower ability pupils. A number of teachers did not perceive the learning processes inherent in the Northern Ireland Curriculum as entirely appropriate for all pupils and referred quite often to the didactic or "chalk and talk" approach prominent in many schools which, according to one teacher *"clearly doesn't capture every pupil's imagination"*.

One teacher discussing the relationship of teachers and pupils, pointed to what she thought might be a fundamental requirement for entering the teaching profession - a liking for children. She commented,

It's frightening you know, but there are a significant number of teachers who don't like children. I can't help but wonder what effects this has on their teaching, not to mention the children's learning.

Relationships between teachers

Throughout the interviews, it became clear that teachers experienced very different relationships with their colleagues. This was dependent on the size of school, the nature of the departments within schools, whether it was a primary, special, integrated or post-primary school and also the culture of the staffroom.

As well as considering the opportunities for formal liaison, teachers also reflected on the nature of informal, everyday relationships in their schools. From the sample of teachers interviewed, primary school teachers seemed to experience much more contact with other members of staff on both a formal and social basis. Many spoke of *"freely walking in and out of each others' rooms"*, *"pooling resources"* and socialising together outside school. Some post-primary teachers echoed these comments, however others intimated that they rarely left their rooms or that they could teach a whole day and have only limited superficial contact with a few teachers. Respondents frequently spoke of a *"seige mentality"*, suggesting that teachers felt imprisioned and under threat from *"just about everyone and everything"*. One teacher commented that often a teacher's first actions on moving into a new classroom was to cover up any windows or glass in the door in order to *"make sure nobody can see what's going on"*.

The style of leadership adopted by the head teacher was perceived as having an influential effect on staff morale and the "collegiate atmosphere" in a school. Teachers referred to different *"types"* of head teacher and the effects they had on staff cohesion, staff communication and individual staff teaching. Several teachers described their principals as living in *"ivory towers"* or *"splendid isolation,"* set apart from other staff members and *"caught up in his own concerns"*. Some principals were considered unapproachable and in these schools teachers explained that problems or concerns were either not voiced or other members of senior management were approached instead. The converse of this situation was described by another teacher,

> *Our head's door is always open. I don't remember ever being turned away. What I find so good is that she remembers what it was like to teach.*

This point was reiterated by other teachers who concluded that once a head teacher became a manager he or she *"becomes locked into a different agenda"*.

The practice of holding regular staff meetings was generally regarded as positive and beneficial, however teachers did feel that the benefit of meetings was conditional on the level of communication, the extent to which teachers had a voice and the degree to which principals and senior management would actively listen. Teachers commented on the importance of daily staff meetings for providing information on whole school issues, pupil absences and where appropriate, individual pupils' problems or situations. This encouraged the staff to work collectively in dealing with pupils and to share responsibility.

However teachers had mixed views in their assessment of whether meetings and formal discussions actually promoted a sense of community. Many admitted that often the most open and invaluable exchanges occurred when *"teachers get together over a cup of coffee without any senior teachers"*.

Several principals acknowledged that,

The staffroom is for the teachers. I tend to avoid it at lunchtimes because the staff like to talk without my spectre looming over them.

Giving staff space to exchange views and opinions was perceived as an integral element of effective management, though teachers and principals were concerned that opportunities for dialogue were used effectively and constructively. According to a large number of respondents, too many times staffroom dialogues degenerated into a *"series of moans and winges"*, *"a diatribe of abuse directed at one pupil"* or *"general griping sessions"*. A few teachers intimated that their school policies had addressed this situation and attempted to heighten teachers' awareness of the negative repercussions such discussions could have on staff morale.

Teachers were asked to comment on how staff interact with one other, for example how they greeted each other in the corridors. Teachers gave a variety of responses. In most cases, they addressed each other using their Christian names, but referred to senior management and the principal using their title and surname. In a minority of schools everyone was addressed using their surname. Some teachers, (in large post-primary schools) admitted that it was quite usual for teachers to ignore each other in the corridor and indeed quite unusual for the principal to address staff. A few teachers did observe, that despite the inclusion of an objective in their school policies (at the request of the Principal) for the promotion of polite and cordial exchange, the principal himself tended to either grunt or ignore staff and pupils when they met in the school.

The values communicated by senior management in the formulation of school policies and timetables, and the nature of relationships were readily identified by most teachers. From their responses, the attitudes and goals of senior management impacted to varying degrees on their perspectives of pupils and their teaching practice. One teacher reflected,

I used to hold sort of tutorials for my weaker pupils, but the VP told me I was wasting my time... and you know, you lose heart... I mean, what's it all about anyway?

Many teachers commented on differences between the culture of maintained and controlled schools, and grammar and secondary schools. The *"traditional"* perception of controlled schools was of a greater emphasis on industry, academic achievement and exams. Maintained schools were regarded as being more concerned with pastoral care, ethos and changing the *"state of things"*. Several respondents suggested however that a number of maintained grammar schools were shifting their ethos, adopting the culture of industry associated with grammar schools. The perceived contrast between grammar and secondary school culture was not entirely different to the controlled/maintained distinction, though there was a perception that considerably more energy and imagination was involved in building pupils' confidence and promoting a sense of worth and value in secondary schools. In general teachers expressed a need for,

> *more time to reflect on school values and priorities and working through the implications of these in practice.*

The parent - teacher relationship

It seemed clear that primary school teachers had much more contact with parents and in some schools, parents actually helped as classroom assistants with lower primary classes. This arrangement worked well where parents undertook a complementary role, providing teachers with support and affording them opportunities to provide more one-to-one teaching. Only a few teachers had encountered problems with *"over enthusiastic"* or *"particularly domineering mothers"*. This co-operative strategy also gave teachers an opportunity to gain some insight into their pupils' home backgrounds.

According to teachers, such experience in the classroom brought parents *"more up to date"* with what was going on in school, and for some, removed the *"fear"* of the teacher and the education system. Teachers remarked that as pupils progressed to the post-primary stage many parents became increasingly reluctant to visit schools or to contact teachers regarding their children's work or progress. This was attributed in some cases to the fact that parents could not identify with just one teacher and in others to parents themselves having had negative experiences of second-level education.

The concept of an "open door" culture appeared to be an important one for parents. Teachers alluded to the school's relationship with parents on many occasions, commenting on the school policy regarding parental access. Some schools, notably smaller schools and primary schools, appeared to welcome parents at almost any time. Others opted for an appointment procedure. Some teachers were suspicious of parents and some described a minority of parents as *"disruptive"*, *"interfering"* and *"mischievious"*. Teachers also expressed disappointment, concern and at times anger over what they perceived in some instances as inadequate parenting or a lack of parental concern. Several agreed that school was a *"safe haven"* for many children, and provided perhaps a rare element of stability and security in their lives. They admitted that the habit of labelling children according to their home background exists in many schools. Despite some concerns over parental care, they agreed that the majority of parents, regardless of their backgrounds, demonstrated a natural concern for their children's educational progress.

Ambiguity and uncertainity about the teacher's role was widely recognised as not only challenging to the individual teacher's position, but also to the whole nature of the school as an autonomous institution. Teachers mentioned on many occasions the expectations of parents and the wider society for them to adopt something of a quasi-parental role. Teachers questioned how far they could adopt this role. In particular, they were concerned as to what extent they could be regarded as *"maintainers of law"*, *"social skills tutors"* and *"moral arbiters."* The majority of teachers readily accepted some responsibility for the social development of their pupils. Indeed many identified this as an inherent requirement of their teaching role. However, quite a number were more reluctant to identify their task in moral terms. Responsibility for teaching rules and regulations or a prescribed moral code was considered by most teachers to be *"beyond the call of duty"* and *"not an entirely appropriate task"*. Teachers often felt this was essentially a parental duty and something which they were not confident with or qualified to undertake.

The practice of devolving responsibility to teachers for pupils' moral, disciplinary and social upbringing was further complicated by the accompanying pressures of accountability. Teachers commented on the publication of league tables, the introduction of parental choice and a perceived strengthening of parents' role in governing bodies. This, they felt, allowed parents a deeper insight into schools and could lead in some respondents' minds at least, to *"potentially dangerous interference"* and *"damaging repercussions"*. Many respondents, speaking as parents themselves, acknowledged the importance of all parents being informed about their children's progress and development, as well as the teaching methods and resources employed by teachers. They also acknowledged the need for parents to have a voice. Alongside this however, were feelings of irritation and anger, and a sense that teachers' *"professional expertise"* was being questioned and increasingly challenged.

The relationship between parent and teacher was commonly characterised as one which is chequered with misunderstanding, misconceptions and differences of opinion. Teachers frequently drew attention to the difficulties of a dichotomy between parents' desire to have a say in their children's education and teachers' desires to cherish and protect their own expertise. The increasing difficulties in this relationship, according to many teachers, had their origins in the *"changing nature of society"* and a perceived shift in family and institutional values and attitudes. Many teachers did feel that they were cast in an *"impossible role"* which expected them to *"fill in all the social, emotional and moral gaps"* and be *"all things to all pupils"*.

The relationship between school and community

The term 'community' is imprecise although it was common in this study for respondents to use it to refer to clergy, local parishes, parents of pupils, School Governors, Parent Teachers Associations (PTAs) and members of local residential and business communities. In a broader sense, community also referred to the rather more generic concept of 'society'. Throughout the interviews, teachers were asked to examine the nature of the relationship which exists between their school and the community and to reflect on the values which framed and underlined these relationships.

Many teachers created the impression of a very close and active relationship between their school and the community in which it was located. Schools had established varying degrees of contact with local people through invitations from the school to share in events, such as open nights, concerts and fund-raising activities. Many examples were also provided of how scientific, social, historical, geographical and environmental aspects of the local area around schools had been integrated into pupils' studies through the curriculum. Pupils had visited local dolmens and ruins, undertaken various studies of local traffic and businesses and met with local poets, storytellers and community figures. A few teachers remarked that studies of the local environment also offered opportunities for the consideration of various moral, religious and ethical themes and EMU was mentioned on many occasions as a vehicle for promoting a greater awareness of community, both locally and further afield. Focusing attention on the local community was also recognised as a way of valuing pupils' own experiences as part of their educational development.

Several teachers spoke of an *"inextricable link"* with the community through religious, political and social networks. Many teachers in maintained schools were very conscious of the place of the school within the parish community, where individuals are linked not only by church membership, but also by common religious, political and social ideas and beliefs. Teachers in rural and urban maintained schools referred to the integral role of the parish priest and church and youth club leaders in shaping values within their schools. A few teachers intimated how the political interests and allegiances of the local community were a strong influence on the daily lessons and activities undertaken in school. They commented on the importance of a consolidated staff approach in dealing with political and sectarian issues and their impact on school life. The conflict in Northern Ireland has evidently made an impact upon many schools, though only a small number of teachers made explicit reference to it. Their schools tended to be located in *"politically sensitive"* areas. Some had taken a decision to ignore local politics or at least to debar them from the school community and others commented that the ceasefires which existed whilst this research was undertaken had, *"served to dispel some of the difficulties which teachers have previously had to cope with"*.

Teachers acknowledged that violence and sectarian divisions in communities of which their schools were a part, posed serious problems at times. They emphasised the value of supportive and cohesive staff relationships, and a public declaration that *"No politics are permitted past the school gate"*.

Teachers in some schools talked about the regular contact they have with social, community and care workers. In areas of high unemployment and social deprivation, teachers indicated that they received support from a range of local people. One primary school teacher illustrated this point by describing an arrangement she had with a local leisure centre. Several of her pupils were not able, for a variety of reasons, to obtain swimming costumes for their weekly PE lesson. Recognising this, the leisure centre staff had provided the children with swimming costumes (and indeed, some other items of clothing) from the long-term lost property box. She concluded,

It's this sort of thoughtfulness and co-operation that reminds you that the school is part of a bigger, caring community.

Special school teachers concluded that close relationships with the local community were not just a valuable asset, but an essential and intrinsic aspect of their pedagogy. Teachers commented that they communicated with a large number personnel and availed of a broad range of services. This list included music, art and drama therapists, dance companies, musicians, clergy, further education colleges, local employers and various charitable bodies.

The transition for pupils, from school to employment, was an issue raised by a large number of teachers. They drew attention to the principles of industry and the emphasis placed on these by teachers in their classrooms. Respondents referred to the *"age-old carrot dangled before pupils"* promising that *"if they work hard, they will do well"*. One teacher suggested that this carrot was *"beginning to rot"* and another asserted that, *"teachers have been preaching this for years, but in today's society, it just doesn't hold water anymore"*.

Preparation for employment (or strategies for dealing with unemployment) were felt to be inadequate and even non-existant in some schools. Teachers thought that there was insufficient contact between schools and employers and that pupils did not learn enough about the *"culture of work"*.

As well as the positive aspects of community relationships, teachers also spoke of the pressures they experienced from the wider society. Issues relating to accountability arose and teachers were unanimous in their outrage at what they described as *"society's readiness to blame teachers for all social and moral ills"*. However, teachers also expressed concern about what they described as their *"diminishing role as educators"* and the increasing expectations for them to accept greater responsibility for more aspects of pupils' development, and to assume an *in loco parentis* role.

Conclusion

A study of the hidden curriculum with respondents uncovered a rich assortment of experiences, relationships and situations underpinned or strongly influenced by a diversity of values, beliefs and attitudes. Many teachers had adopted the term "ethos" to describe or represent what they knowingly or otherwise recognised as the hidden curriculum in their schools. The values and principles which teachers (usually senior management) identified in their policies as "pervading school life" were frequently recognised as the "school ethos". Comments about the triangular relationship between teachers, pupils and parents provided a valuable insight into the type of implicit value-laden messages transmitted within the school, and between the school, home and community. What emerged forcibly from these messages was a profound concern over the changing role of teachers and the ever-increasing demands which they felt were being placed upon them. This was coupled with a recognition of the significance of community and the need to cultivate a sense of collegiality within the school while also developing close and sustained links with a wide range of institutions in the local and wider communities.

Chapter seven

Summary and recommendations

This report was commissioned by the Northern Ireland Council for the Curriculum, Examinations and Assessment (CCEA) to identify current initiatives and approaches to values education; to investigate teachers' perceptions of values within the Northern Ireland Curriculum; and to suggest possible ways in which the development of a values dimension might inform the next review of the Northern Ireland Curriculum in the year 2001. The report is summarised below under three main headings:

Current values initiatives

This element of the report provides:

*   a description of different education initiatives concerning values and education in Europe, the UK and Northern Ireland (pages 13-32);

*   a comprehensive list of organisations involved in values education or concerned with values in education (Appendix 3, pages 127-142);

*   an extensive bibliography of relevant literature (pages 145-162).

The main points arising from this part of the investigation are:

i.   The emphasis on values in education in the UK has been effected mainly by a range of voluntary agencies which have sought to influence statutory education bodies. Many of these organisations have come together under the umbrella of a recently-established Values Education Council.

ii.   Scotland is an exception in that the Scottish Consultative Council for the Curriculum (SCCC) has given this area considerable prominence in its mission statement and publications. The Gordon Cook Foundation (also based in Scotland) has played a significant role in funding the work of voluntary, statutory and academic agencies in this area.

iii. Recent political debate in England has raised questions about the role of education in relation to a perceived moral decline within society and greater attention is currently being given to this area by statutory bodies. The School Assessment and Curriculum Authority (SCAA) produced a discussion paper on the spiritual and moral development of young people in July 1996 and set up the National Forum for Values in Education and the Community to consult widely on the degree of consensus concerning the values which schools might promote. Statements from the Secretary of State for Education suggest that some consideration is being given to the introduction of specific programmes for Citizenship and/or Social and Moral Education to the statutory curriculum.

iv. The review of current initiatives as part of this study revealed a variety of approaches including philosophical studies, curriculum guidance and resources, publications directed towards teachers many with examples of 'good practice', training materials and numerous research and development projects, reports and articles. Overall these represent a substantial, but largely disparate body of knowledge and experience.

v. The main frustration for those working within this area appears to be how this body of knowledge and practice can be drawn together in a coherent way and made available to pupils. This raises questions about the lack of integration between the approaches developed by individual projects and the framework for the Northern Ireland Curriculum; and about the capacity of teachers to integrate such approaches into their teaching in a routine and practical way.

vi. Progress in this area is complicated by an ideological rift. It is characterised by a distinction between the use of the term *Values Education* which many take to mean a form of Moral Education that advocates the teaching of a prescribed or explicit moral code, and *Values in Education* which may be associated with moral enquiry but also refers to a broader set of concerns such as school ethos, discipline, behaviour and relationships within the school.

Teacher perspectives on values within the NI Curriculum

These sections of the report are based on a series of interviews involving more than 60 teachers, Principals and education Advisers and provide a detailed account of their perceptions of values under the following headings:

- the *formal* curriculum in terms of Areas of Study (pages 33-72) and Cross Curricular Themes (pages 72-80);

- the *informal* curriculum in terms of aspects of school life such as extra-curricular activities, school assemblies, school policies and pastoral care (pages 85-98);

- the *hidden* curriculum in terms of school ethos, the organisation of learning and various relationships within the school (pages 99-114).

The main points to emerge were as follows:

i. The research confirmed that most teachers recognise that values are inherent in the formal, informal and hidden curriculum, however, few teachers could identify how an explicit consideration of values informs their daily preparation for teaching;

ii. The majority of teachers were concerned that any attempts to give greater prominence to values in education should be done through the existing curriculum framework and not become an added imposition;

iii. The research identified teachers' concerns about an over-emphasis on cognitive dimensions of the curriculum and a recognition that the social and emotional development of young people are important elements of the education process which merit more considered attention;

iv. The research identified a suspicion on the part of some teachers that the development of values in education might mean that they are asked to promote a prescribed code of moral behaviour. There is deep resistance to such an approach amongst many teachers. It will therefore be important to provide clear guidance which distinguishes between moral education and broader approaches involving values clarification and enquiry.

Strengthening values within curriculum

Whilst there has not been an explicit or statutory approach to values in education in Northern Ireland, the research identified an awareness amongst teachers of many value-related issues which arise through their teaching of the formal curriculum and cross curricular themes. It also became clear that values have a considerable influence in determining many characteristics of school life including the overall ethos and nature of relationships within the school. A common criticism from teachers is that the process and pace of Education Reform has led to a preoccupation with curriculum content and the cognitive development of pupils to the detriment of concerns for the personal, social, moral and emotional development of young people. It is therefore unsurprising that few teachers could state that they had given considered thought and reflection to the values dimension of their teaching in recent years. Despite this, the vast majority of teachers recognised the critical importance of a broad and balanced education and seemed supportive of the notion that the area of values should receive more attention.

The outcomes of this investigation suggest that, in order to strengthen the values dimension of the curriculum, further developments need to take place in the following areas:

1. Better definition of the field

    The area of values and their influence on the education process is conceptually complex. Whilst there is a broad body of practice, teachers will need support to navigate their way around the variety of approaches which are available. In particular, the distinction between moral education and moral enquiry needs careful consideration.

    Presently the debate in Britain seems to be leading towards the emergence of a curriculum area concerned with Social and Moral Education with a strong emphasis on Citizenship. In the Republic of Ireland the area is most strongly focused through the recent introduction of Civic, Social and Political Education. Neither seem to define the area precisely in terms of Northern Ireland needs which appear to relate more to areas of 'personal and social development' and specific concerns that there may be a need for some form of 'political education' or 'education for democratic citizenship'.

It is clear that more widespread debate and discussion will be necessary over the coming years for the area to become better defined. This will become increasingly important as the system approaches the next curriculum review in 2001.

2. Better integration within the curriculum

One of the most common frustrations for teachers in relation to the values dimension is a perceived lack of integrity with existing curriculum frameworks. For many teachers they simply do not see how or where this work can be incorporated into their teaching. Assuming it will be possible to define the area more precisely a number of strategies for better integration into the curriculum exist:

i. *infusion* - this approach is based on the idea that the values inherent in the teaching of every subject are given more conscious attention and a consideration of values is brought to the forefront of the teaching process. Such an approach would necessitate a major reconstruction of every subject in the curriculum, but its virtue would be the highest possible degree of integrity between curriculum subjects and a concern for values. An example of this approach is the Nuffield curriculum in Design and Technology.

ii. *permeation* - this approach seeks to influence the attention given to values across the range of subject areas. It already exists to the extent that the NI Curriculum has six cross curricular themes. Its weakness is that individual teachers do not necessarily identify with a responsibility to promote the area and recent research has questioned the visibility of cross curricular themes at classroom level. Of the current themes, Education for Mutual Understanding and Health Education would seem to be most closely identified with a values dimension, however it may be confusing to concentrate a values dimension through a mechanism that has questionable impact. For the same reason, teachers did not respond positively to the notion of a new cross curricular theme related specifically to values education.

iii. *a timetabled programme* - this approach would seek to strengthen the values dimension through an already existing subject, such as Religious Education, or develop a separate programme of study which would be introduced into the timetabled curriculum. Many teachers felt that the former approach already existed but was limited by the extent to which it concentrated solely on a particular set of Christian values and also had the disadvantage that it enabled other teachers to absolve themselves from responsibility for the work. The development of a new programme within the school timetable raised anxieties about the space for such work within an already crowded timetable and who would teach the programme. However, it was widely accepted that the main advantage would be the potential impact of recognised space for the work to take place.

3. Raising awareness at whole school level

It is clear that the pervasive nature of values extends beyond the formal curriculum. This study has highlighted aspects of the informal and hidden curriculum which may have significant influence in determining the learning environment. Such aspects include the values communicated through extra-curricular activities, school assemblies, discipline and pastoral policies, the physical environment and the nature of relationships within the school. It is clear that any approach through the formal curriculum needs to be complemented by an awareness of the values communicated by the school by less visible factors. Raising awareness at this level will necessarily involve staff development on issues related to values which affect the whole school.

4. Assessment

Many teachers drew attention to the low status which might be conferred on this area of work because it is not assessed formally. However, opinion on evaluation and assessment seems divided and there are also those who claim that it is inappropriate to assess children's development in this area. An important distinction needs to be made between the actual values which young people hold and any assessment of young people's learning about values. There was a broad consensus that the teacher has a responsibility to raise pupils' awareness about the range of values within society, but this does not confer a moral authority to make judgements about the values held by individual pupils. Some teachers thought it should be possible to assess the quality of pupils' learning, for example through continuous assessment or project work.

5. Personal and professional development of teachers

Of necessity, in recent years, teachers have been preoccupied with Education Reform and the content of new Programmes of Study. This has left little opportunity for reflection upon values and how they are communicated through the education process. Irrespective of how an engagement with values can be strengthened through the curriculum, any strategy will only succeed to the extent that measures are put in place to support teachers' capacity to undertake the work. In practice this means creating more opportunities for teachers to reflect on their own values and the implications for their professional role as a teacher. This needs to be a recurring experience which takes place at succeeding stages throughout a teacher's career. Presently this would mean that specific attention would need to be given to values in professional development programmes for teachers at the following levels:

- initial teacher training
- induction during the initial years of teaching
- early in-service and professional development
- advanced professional development (including research studies)
- senior management training

Recommendations

A developmental approach

The position of values within the debate about Social and Moral Education and Citizenship is still taking place in Britain. Within the Republic of Ireland a similar debate has been resolved through the introduction of Civic, Social and Political Education into the formal curriculum. Whilst elements from both jurisdictions may inform discussions about values in relation to the curriculum, it is clear that there are concerns distinctive to Northern Ireland. It is therefore recommended that a developmental approach is adopted for this work leading up the next review of the Northern Ireland Curriculum in 2001. In practice this means using the intervening years to address many of the issues mentioned above. In essence it would mean taking a holistic view of what will be required to raise awareness of and provide greater prominence for a consideration of values as an integral part of the curriculum.

In practice it is recommended that a significant period of further development work within the system takes place on three broad fronts:

1. *Better curricular definition* of the area needs to be undertaken in close consultation with practitioners. An inclusive approach should be adopted. Initiatives to integrate a values dimension within individual subjects should be encouraged; the values dimension to cross-curricular themes should be strengthened; and there should be some exploration of a specific programme which might become incorporated into the curriculum at a future date.

2. *Development of pilot programmes* should be undertaken so that the work is grounded in practice. The period 1997-98 offers an opportunity for resource development and planning for pilot programmes at each Key Stage which could be tested over three school years (1998-99, 1999-00 and 2000-01). The system would then be better placed to decide where this work sits within the curriculum as part of the Northern Ireland Curriculum Review in 2001.

3. *Personal and professional development of teachers.* The capacity of teachers to integrate a values dimension into their teaching may prove to be one of the most important factors in determining the impact of incorporating this work into the Northern Ireland Curriculum. It will therefore be essential to influence the prominence and attention which is given to values as part of the education process at all training and professional development levels (including initial teacher training, induction, in-service, advanced professional development studies and senior management training). The possibilities for practical programmes should be discussed with providers at all these levels.

Appendix 1

Interview schedule

Teaching experience and practice

- Could you briefly outline your teaching background and experience?

- What are your present responsibilities in your school/post?

- What teaching methods do you use?

- Describe the nature of classroom management which you employ.

- What skills/abilities are promoted through this subject? How would you seek to promote these?

- Do you think there are there any instances where (your subject area) may overlap with any other subjects?

- What would you identify as your main concerns with (your subject area) in the curriculum?

Values and subject area

- How do you feel this subject features as part of the whole curriculum?

- How is (your subject area) perceived by your head teacher/other teachers/ parents in your school?

- What would you identify as "value-laden" issues within this subject area?

- How would you approach these issues in class?

- What opportunities are you afforded to teach controversial issues?

- What values issues have you encountered within the cross-curricular themes?

- What would you identify as the major skills/qualities of a good teacher in your subject area?

Values and Education

- What are your initial responses to the concept of values in the Northern Ireland curriculum?

- How/where would you identify values in the formal curriculum?

- Do you feel it is possible to teach and give nothing of yourself?

- To what extent to you feel you communicate your own personal views in class?

- What values would you say are embodied or promoted in your school?

- How are policies formulated and implemented in your school?

Values and Teaching

- How would you define your role as a teacher?

- What expectations do you feel are upon you as a teacher in your school?

- How would you describe the nature of relationships between teachers in your school?

- What are your concerns about teaching in the 1990s?

Appendix 2

CIDREE guidelines on values

Recommendations For The Humanistic And International Dimension Of Education (CIDREE, pp. 39-44)

Schools should support the development of the humanistic and international dimension of education by promoting in all pupils:

*   independence of mind
*   consideration for others
*   a sense of fairness, together with a respect for justice and the rights of others
*   respect for ways of life, opinions and ideas different from one's own, provided they are based on consideration for others
*   a sense of decency
*   a commitment to the promotion of democratic processes
*   a concern for the well-being of themselves, other individuals and society.

These objectives present challenges and opportunities for schools in a number of ways:

*   at the level of school policies
*   classroom climate
*   in the learning and teaching process
*   in the pastoral care system
*   in the physical environment of the school
*   in the planned curriculum.

Practical suggestions for the implementation of the guidelines

School Policies

These should:

• recognise the importance of the values dimension in all aspects of the curriculum
• be collaboratively planned with all staff
• develop staff understanding
• be monitored for effectiveness
• be reviewed regularly

Comment: This means fostering a management style that points up the importance of collaboration, positive and supportive relationships, consensus building and consistent monitoring and evaluation procedures.

Classroom Climate

Every classroom should reflect:

• respect for each individual
• respect for self
• respect for a variety of cultures
• a sense of belonging to the community of the classroom
• caring, consideration, empathy
• co-operative working skills
• learner autonomy
• appreciation of learning
• rights, responsibilities and rules
• a continuing evaluation and development of the classroom climate
• trust, a sense of valuing the individual
• the joy of learning

Comment: This means planning and developing a climate where both the learning/teaching process and the hidden curriculum of interpersonal relationships:

- promote effective learning for all
- stimulate individual progress
- respond to individual aspirations
- encourage openness and negotiation
- allow pupils to take responsibility for their own learning

The Teaching/Learning Process

The teaching/learning process should be:

- active
- participative
- investigative
- varied
- co-operative
- supportive
- learner-centred
- differentiated

It should encourage:

- independent learning
- personal autonomy
- critical thinking
- self-esteem
- investigation
- imagination
- creativity
- the construction of knowledge in terms of information, concepts, skills, attitudes and values

Comment: This means devising strategies and approaches that encourage and validate the contribution of all learners. It also means providing educational experiences that develop and extend the learners' interests and enthusiasm along with the capacity for critical reflection.

Pastoral Care

The Pastoral Care system should:

- value each learner
- build supportive relationships
- promote the school as a secure educational base
- encourage discussion and negotiation
- promote partnerships between school, parents and the wider community

Comment: This means promoting trust, caring and a sense of belonging by devising procedures that: allow each learner to develop a supportive relationship with an identified member of staff; develop channels of communication with parents and others in the community; create mechanisms for conflict resolution and for addressing individual anxieties and thus provide a means of promoting the well-being of all pupils.

Physical Environment

This should:

- promote a sense of well-being
- stimulate
- be welcoming, comfortable, colourful, attractive and ever changing

Comment: This means taking every opportunity to promote a welcoming and reassuring atmosphere in the school and its classrooms. This can be achieved through:

- welcoming signs and notices
- displays and exhibitions of work
- recognition of cultural and ethnic diversity
- warm and responsive interpersonal communications
- attention to the impact of the physical environment
- care for the fabric and condition of the buildings.

Appendix 3

Values education - organisations and projects

UK ORGANISATIONS

Centre for Alleviating Social Problems through Values Education (CAVE)
aims to enhance the quality of life by initiating practical values education
development programmes in schools and youth organisations, publishing
research and examples of good practice and lobbying government officials.

Centre for Citizenship Studies in Education
assists schools in implementing citizenship education by providing information,
in-service training, and school products. The Centre also generates publications
and holds a resource and bibliography database.

Centre for Values Education for Life
aims to advance the education of young people through provision of moral,
social, personal and health education through small project groups consisting
of disadvantaged 10-18 year olds.

Centre for Religious Education Development and Research (CREDAR)
is based at the School of Education, University of Birmingham. The Centre
promotes research and curriculum development in all aspects of religious
education, worship and faith development. Studies have been undertaken into
primary RE, the effectiveness of teacher training in RE and the evaluation of
attainment targets in RE.

Christian Education Movement (CEM)
promotes research and development in education, in particular Religious
Education through publications and professional development.

Citizenship Foundation (The)
"seeks to improve and extend the quality of citizenship, particularly through
education". In pursuit of this aim, the Foundation undertakes a variety of
activities including research, school competitions, consultancy and training. It

has also produced a range of curriculum materials addressing issues such as human rights, consumerism and moral and social development.

Community Education Development Centre (CEDC)
provides training, support, consultancy through the publication and dissemination of resources, projects and curriculum materials on citizenship and community enterprise education.

Gordon Cook Foundation (The)
is a charitable organisation which seeks to promote and advance "all aspects of education which are likely to [further] character development and citizenship". To this end, the Foundation has funded and supported many research and development projects and activities perceived to be within the realm of values education. Such projects have included the preparation and piloting of values education materials for primary schools, investigations into young people's and parental values, and the role of the media in values education. [A more comprehensive list of projects supported by the Gordon Cook Foundation is listed below]. The Foundation has also supported projects on values or values education in individual schools, conferences, workshops, training courses, and the production of publications and curriculum materials in association with other agencies.

Projects sponsored solely or partly by the Gordon Cook Foundation

Developing a Whole School Values Ethos: A Headteacher's Guide
Developing Teacher Initiatives in Values Education
Guidelines for Headteachers on Whole School Approach to values education
Parent Conceptions of Values and Values Education
Progressing Values Education in England, Wales and Northern Ireland
Research on Values Education (ROVE)
Role of the teacher and the Hidden Curriculum
School Values and Ethos Project
The Philosophy of Values and Values Education
The Role of the Media in Values Education
The Values in Business Education in Schools Project
Transmission of Values in pre-school environment
Values Education: A Resource book based on Reading 360
Values Education: Making a Start (video)
Values Education in the Primary School
Values Education Resource Pack for Trainers in Girl Guides

Values in Children's Personal Reading
Values in Education: an industrial approach
Values in Further Education
Values in Liberal Education and Vocational Training Initiatives
Values in Primary Education
Values in the Playground
Values Education in the Secondary School

Institute for Citizenship Studies (The)
encourages active citizenship by educating children and training adults and clarifying the law. The Institute produces teaching materials and organises seminars, meetings and competitions.

Moral and Social Action Interdisciplinary Colloquium (MOSAIC)
is an international cross-disciplinary colloquium of researchers and practitioners in moral development and education and values issues. Holds an annual workshop conference and provides networking.

Multicultural Education after ERA:Concerns and Challenges for the 1990s
is a project examining the values underpinning the Educational Reform Act 1988 (ERA), in particular issues relating to the realisation of equal opportunities and the translation of multicultural anti-racist policies into practice. Diagnostic and responsive in nature the project sought to establish current concerns among local education authorities and identify possible developmental strategies.

National Association Pastoral Care in Education (NAPCE)
promotes understanding, research and training in pastoral care for schools through publications and national events.

NAVET
is The National Association for Values Education and Training. This body focuses on the understanding and communication of values and their application within education and training. It produces a regular newsletter, *NewsValues* and publishes series of short papers, entitled the *NAVET* papers.

Norham Foundation (The)
aims to promote morality in every aspect of community life. It offers training programmes in moral education, counselling, gender and PSE and provides curriculum development in PSE. Action research has also been undertaken into

a *Just School* project which examines possible ways of establishing justice-centred schools. The *Schools and Values Project* is extending this work, by focusing on school development strategies, addressing training and consultation needs and assessing the outcomes, in terms of effects on school curriculum, climate and curriculum development.

Nuffield Foundation (The)
has recently published curriculum materials on design and technology with opportunities for the exploration of associated values issues. The materials have been devised to allow pupils to approach values in three ways, through:
- an appraisal of real life design and technology issues;
- an analysis of values implicit in their own design and construction tasks;
- the identification of positive and negative aspects of design and technology using a 'Winners and Losers' strategy.

Office for Standards in Education (OFSTED)
undertakes inspections and reviews of school standards. "Spiritual, moral, social and cultural development" (SCSC) has been outlined as one of four statutory elements outlined for inspection in OFSTED's *Framework for Inspection* (1993) and values have been contextualised within this framework.

RIMSCUE
The Centre for Research into Moral, Spiritual and Cultural Understanding and Education has undertaken research into areas such as the moral, spiritual and cultural development of children, ethos, the hidden curriculum and values in education.

Schools Curriculum and Assessment Authority (SCAA)
has produced a series of discussion papers and reports on values and moral and spiritual development. These include, *Spiritual and Moral Development* and *Education for Adult Life: The Spiritual Development of Young People*. SCAA intends that these documents be used to promote understanding and discussion and to inform future development of these areas in schools.

Scottish Consultative Council for the Curriculum (SCCC)
has indicated a strong commitment to the promotion and development of values in education throughout the curriculum. The council has addressed values in the context of the whole curriculum and produced a range of discussion documents, and resources for the classroom and staffroom.

Scottish Council for Research in Education (SCRE)
is an independent body which conducts and communicates research to support policy-making and practice in Scottish Education. Research projects have addressed school development planning, discipline and Values Education in Primary Schools.

Social Values Research Centre
identifies as its key objective the promotion of informed discussion of social values in relation to contemporary problems. Personal relationships in education, education in a plural society, ethical and social issues have been explored through various publications.

Values Education Council (VEC)
has been established to promote dialogue on values and their "application in education and society", to provide a network to facilitate the exchange of information, to provide a "framework within which council members can work together with those in public policy in education" and to support those involved in the whole field of values education.

VECTOR
Values Education, Consultancy, Training and Organisational Research provides information on values education, identifies and disseminated examples of good practice in values education, pursues training and organisational development opportunities and supports a network of interested bodies through the publication of a regular newsletter,

UK PROJECTS

Adolescent Values in Comparative Cultures
is ongoing research work based at the University of Loughborough, which aims to develop an understanding of adolescent values in comparative cultures, (Japanese, Saudi-Arabian, Israeli-Arab).

A Moralist Realist Approach to Moral Education
is an individual research project underway at Westminster College, Oxford. The research is essentially a philosophical inquiry into the possibility of objectivity in moral judgement, looking in particular at theories in moral realism and the role of knowledge and reason in moral education.

Clarifying the distinctive contribution of Christianity to Values Education in the Junior School
is a curriculum development project examining teachers' perceptions, understanding and communication of Christian values. The project intends to provoke teachers' thinking at initial and in-service training about the distinctive elements of Christian values and how they might help pupils to reflect on the contribution of Christian beliefs to values.

Ethos Indicators in Primary and Secondary School Self-evaluation
were developed by the Management of Education Resources (MERU) within HMI in Scotland. A set of twelve ethos indicators was developed which could then be used by schools to evaluate their own effectiveness and quality. The instruments comprised alternative forms of questionnaires for pupils, teachers and parents and interviews for younger children and pupils with special needs. Quite a number of schools have engaged in this process of self-evaluation in Scotland, and then sought ways to integrate the indicators instrument within their school development programmes.

Human Rights Education Materials for the Primary School
is a set of cross-curricular materials developed at the Centre for Global Education in York. Specific games and activities are included facilitating a study of human rights at a local and global level.

Just School Project
is part of the work of The Norham Foundation. (See above).

Learning and Teaching Values in Nurseries
is a research project using case studies of staff perceptions and practice, and a photographic analysis of values in nurseries. The work is focused on one Local Education Authority in Scotland.

National Forum for Values in Education in the Community
was set up by SCAA during 1996. The Forum consisted of 150 people and was asked *to consult widely on ways in which schools might be supported in making a contribution to pupils' spiritual, moral, social and cultural development* and *to what extent there is any agreement on the values, attitudes and behaviour that schools should promote on society's behalf.* The Forum will reconvene in January 1997 to consider the results of the consultation process.

Personal, Social, Moral and Religious Education in Primary Schools.
'The impact and implications of the Education Reform Act 1988 and the National Curriculum' is a piece of research which examines four interconnected areas of the curriculum, providing insights into their place and purpose in the primary curriculum. The nature of the four subject areas, implications and effects of the Education Reform Act and national curriculum, and the interconnective nature of these subject areas are considered in greater depth.

Programme for Education in Citizenship
is based at the Institute for Education, University of London, this programme aims to promote research, publication and postgraduate study on education for citizenship with values education as a major component.

Role of the teacher and the hidden curriculum
is a research project which identified a two-fold purpose of discovering more about teachers' own opinions on and attitudes to values education and providing them with conceptual and other resources to address some of the basic questions. The work was undertaken through the Moray House Institute, Heriot-Watt University, Edinburgh.

School and Values Project
is undertaken under the auspices of The Norham Foundation. (See above).

The Influence of Catholic Schools on pupil attitudes and religious values
is a research project which aims to examine the religious attitudes and values of Catholic/non Catholic pupils educated in Catholic and non-denominational schools in Scotland. The researchers are based at Trinity College, Dyfed.

Towards an Introduction of the Concept of the Whole Child and Well-being
is a doctoral research project examining the implicit and explicit values, and the concepts of autonomy, creativity and well-being within the presentation of health-related exercise in early years education. The project is based at Rolle Faculty of Education in Plymouth.

Understanding Values Education in Primary Schools:
is a research project funded by the Gordon Cook Foundation which aims to explore the values which are implicitly or explicitly taught in Scottish primary schools, to investigate parents', pupils' and teachers' perceptions of values education and to raise awareness about values education.

Values and Visions
is part of the Manchester Development Project and has been developed to "encourage spiritual development and global awareness in the primary school". A major aim of the project is to help schools consider ways in which they might develop an understanding of their own shared values and visions through participation in whole school activities.

Values in Liberal Education and Vocational Training Initiatives
has been undertaken in three separate projects. This research addressed the reconcilation of different values inherent in liberal education and vocational training, a criticism of the market values underpinning educational change and a study of the alternative curriculum based on student-centred values, to reconcile academic and vocational tracks.

NORTHERN IRELAND ORGANISATIONS

All Children Together (ACT)
is the pioneering movement for the development of integrated education in Northern Ireland. It offers advice, holds conferences and seminars, undertakes activities to raise awareness and publishes a newsletter - *ACTLET*.

Community Relations in Schools (CRIS)
provides support for teachers engaged in cross-community contact programmes as part of their work on EMU and Cultural Heritage cross-curricular themes. Amongst other things, it provides advice on planning and resourcing programmes, produces worksheets, organises workshops and supplies extra staff for group activities.

Co-operation North
has as part of its work, the Youth and Education Programme which aims to promote tolerance and understanding between young people from the two traditions within Northern Ireland and between young people in the North and South of Ireland. As well as facilitating an exchange programme in schools as part of its EMU activities, Co-operation North also offers grant aid and training seminars for teachers and Youth workers.

Council for Education and World Citizenship (CEWC)
aims to "build bridges of understanding and co-operation between peoples and

nations." An important aspect of this work is to help young people to become active well-informed citizens. CEWC regularly produces *Broadsheets* which provides information on topical issues for young people. A major aspect of CEWC work in Northern Ireland is the organisation of Senior and Junior conferences on major European or world issues.

Department of Education for Northern Ireland (DENI)
is responsible for the central administration of education in Northern Ireland. It works in partnership with a number of statutory bodies including the five Education and Library Boards, CCMS and NICCEA. In its publication *A Strategic Analysis* under the heading of the aims of the education service, reference is made to the "development of appropriate values and attitudes in school life" and to the aim that "young people...develop the... attitudes and values and motivation they need for their personal and social fulfilment.

Education and Library Boards (ELBs)
Each of the five Education and Library Boards have advisory staff with specific remits for value related areas of the curriculum - EMU, Cultural Heritage, Whole School Issues, RE, PSE and School Management.

Forum on Community Understanding and Schools (FOCUS)
is an informal network of over 30 organisations and individuals working in the area of EMU and Cultural Heritage in schools in Northern Ireland. The group meets to discuss matters of concern and to offer mutual support in this aspect of education.

Northern Ireland Council for Integrated Education (NICIE)
was established to support those wishing to set up integrated schools and those integrated schools already in existence. The integrated ethos constitutes a 60/40 balance in pupils, staff and governance, an all-ability pupil community and a child-centred curriculum, with the aim of maximising the potential of all children in their educational and social development.

Northern Ireland Council for the Curriculum, Examinations and Assessment (NICCEA)
has a number of responsibilities in its remit. These are to:- keep under review all aspects of the curriculum, examinations and assessment for grant-aided schools; to advise DENI on matters concerned with the curriculum, examinations and assessment; to publish and distribute information and to conduct statutory consultations on proposals relating to legislation issues involving the curriculum,

examinations and assessment; and to conduct examinations and assessments. The 'Values in Education' project was commissioned by NICCEA.

Peace and Reconciliation Inter-Schools Movement (PRISM)
aims to break down geographical, denominational and social barriers by providing opportunities for young people to meet and discuss local controversial and divisive issues. The group organises meetings, drama workshops and residentials.

Ulster Folk and Transport Museum
offers teachers opportunities to allow pupils to participate in residential programmes and to engage in practical educational activities relating to EMU and Cultural Heritage. As well as exploring aspects of local history, the programmes promote positive cross community contact.

PROJECTS IN NORTHERN IRELAND

School Bullying Project
is an initiative developed in the North Eastern Education and Library Board as part of its policy on bullying. Workshops and seminars were held, giving guidance on the development of whole school response to bullying. Particular attention was paid to the creation of a positive and accepting school ethos where all children were valued and made aware of their value. Photocopiable resource materials were also made available. Schools involved commented that the sessions were interesting and productive and feedback from pupils was also favourable.

CCMS Whole School Guidance
contains a series of guidelines on the preparation and development of a whole school curriculum policy and school development planning.

Churches Peace Education Programme
was developed under the auspices of the Irish Council of Churches and the Irish Commission for Justice and Peace. The programme has three main features; the production of educational materials, work with teachers, parents, church educators and others to promote education for understanding and peace; and the promotion and dissemination of resources. This has been undertaken through the Peace Education Resources Centre.

Cross Community Contact Scheme
provides funds for projects initiated between two or more schools, where the participants are mixed on a cross-community basis within the ratio 60:40/ 40:60 and the project involves new contacts or the development of existing ones. Projects are also expected to be ongoing, systematic, purposeful and genuinely collaborative.

Dimensions of the Curriculum
was a review exercise undertaken by the Northern Ireland Curriculum Council (NICC) of the physical, cultural, moral, spiritual, intellectual and emotional dimensions of the curriculum. Each area of study was explored through the four Key Stages. Evidence of the developmental dimensions highlighted and concrete examples were cited from the programmes of study.

EMU programmes and courses
Inservice training for EMU and Cultural Heritage is available through the five Education and Library Boards in association with the Regional Training Unit (RTU). The universities also offer modules on EMU as part of the Diploma in Advanced Education (DASE) and the Postgraduate Diploma in Education.

Environment Projects and Programmes
have been undertaken by Advisors with Education and Library boards and by a variety of other voluntary bodies, (some of whom are part of FOCUS; Ulster Wildlife Trust, Speedwell Project, Kilcranny Farm and Slieve Gullion Centre). Activities have centred around raising children and young people's awareness of the values associated with school, community and global environments, and encouraging their participation in a range of curricular and extra-curricular activities.

School Evaluation (WELB)
consists of a number of schools in the Western Education and Library Board who have participated in courses and/or undertaken some form of school evaluation. Some schools participated in the 'Ethos Indicators' Course (entitled School Self-Evaluation for Development Planning) and/or implemented the 'Ethos Indicators' evaluative programme. Several schools undertook an evaluation with the support of the DENI Inspectorate and others developed their own assessment criteria.

European Studies Project
consists of interlinked programmes for pupils aged 11-18 years, which

contribute to the wider dimensions of EMU. Schools can undertake studies into national and international issues using E-mail exchanges, mini company activities, established links with business and commerce and study packs.

Pastoral Issues Courses
have been offered through the Educational and Library Boards and the Regional Training Unit. Summer courses were offered in 'Managing the Pastoral Dimension' at primary and post-primary levels. Participants were presented with a selection of approaches for formulating and implementing pastoral care throughout the school. Materials produced by NAPCE were also provided.

Peer Mediation Programme (The)
aims to promote children's understanding and management of conflict and to encourage and empower them to deal with their own arguments and disagreements. A training process has been established in a number of primary schools in the WELB, giving P7 pupils the opportunity to explore conflict and mediation through a series of workshops. "Elected" mediators have then gone to mediate occurrences of conflict between fellow pupils in the playground and school environment.

Quaker Peace Education Project
was established in 1988 as an action based research project, promoting peace education in schools through a variety of events and activities in collaboration with teachers. This is accompanied by ongoing research into identifying and developing strategies for possible use in peace education. Development work has also been undertaken in selected secondary schools in the WELB. Attempts have been made to improve the quality of relationships between staff and pupils through the provision of a supportive environment and the facilitation of opportunities for positive contact.

Speak Your Piece
is a research and development project funded by the European Community and based within the School of Education at the University of Ulster and involves partnerships with Channel 4 Schools, Ulster Television and the Youth Council for Northern Ireland. The project is concerned with the exploration of controversial issues through schools and youth organisations. A series of five television programmes has been produced and is broadcast by Channel 4. These highlight various controversial issues including identity, politics, religion and culture and aim to raise the level of debate and understanding amongst

14-17 year olds. The project has focused on piloting these programmes with groups of teachers and youth workers and the production of support materials.

Learning Support Initiatives (WELB)
is a curriculum support project involving WELB advisors and centring on the development and use of curricular materials with pupils requiring some form of learning support. The project acknowledges the "special" needs of all individuals and advocates the affirmation of all pupils.

Traveller Project
is being undertaken by three of the Education and Library Boards who have appointed liaison teachers to deal exclusively with traveller children's education. Their remit is to liaise and consult with and provide support for the traveller community, schools, and the department and to disseminate appropriate information to the relevant agencies. One dimension of this work has been to research and disseminate traveller culture and values in order to provide appropriate teacher training and suitable curriculum materials and and to encourage greater understanding and tolerance in the wider educational community.

The Developing School
was introduced in the WELB in September 1995. This project is undertaken within the 'Raising School Standards Initiative' and involves around 20 primary and post-primary schools, invited to participate by DENI. One of the main intentions of the project is to encourage staff to formulate an action plan for their schools and following approval of this plan to provide funding and practical support for its implementation.

The EMU Promoting School Project
aims to promote peer mediation in schools throughout Northern Ireland and assist schools in developing EMU at the heart of the school ethos. Participating schools are encouraged to develop whole school programmes and in-service training is offered to teachers.

The Northern Ireland Curriculum Cohort Study
was commissioned by NICCEA to examine pupils' experiences of the curriculum in terms of its coherence, appropriateness and totality. The pilot phase has recently been completed by the National Foundation for educational Research (NFER) revealing some interesting findings regarding pupils' understanding and perception of values in and across the formal curriculum.

The Strabane Initiative
is a multilateral project based in Strabane. It has been initiated to address areas
of locally identified need in the community and aims to examine all phases of
educational provision from pre-school to further education with the involvement
of parents, teachers, pupils and various statutory and voluntary agencies.

Appendix 4

List of abbreviations

BELB	Belfast Education and Library Board
CAVE	Centre for Alleviating Social Problems through Values Education
CCMS	Catholic Council for Maintained Schools
CEM	Christian Education Movement
CEWC	Council for Education in World Citizenship
CIDREE	Consortium of Institutions for the Development of Research in Education in Europe
CPEP	Churches Peace Education Project
CREDAR	Centre for Religious Education Development and Research
CRIS	Community Relations in Schools
DENI	Department of Education, Northern Ireland
ELB	Education and Library Board
EMU	Education for Mutual Understanding
CH	Cultural Heritage
CCS	Cross-community Contact Scheme
FOCUS	Forum on Community Understanding and Schools
HE	Home Economics
HMI	Her Majesty's Inspectorate (for Schools)
MOSAIC	Moral and Social Interdisciplinary Colloqium
NAPCE	National Association for Pastoral Care in Education
NAVET	National Association for Values Education Training
NEELB	North Eastern Education and Library Board
NI	Northern Ireland
NICC	Northern Ireland Curriculum Council
NICCEA	Northern Ireland Council for the Curriculum, Examinations and Assessment
NICIE	Northern Ireland Council for Integrated Education
NFER	National Foundation for Educational Research
NCC	National Curriculum Council
OFSTED	Office for Standards in Education
PSE	Personal and Social Education

PRISM	Peace and Reconciliation Inter-schools Movement
RE	Religious Education
RIMSCUE	Centre for Research into Moral, Spiritual, and Cultural Understanding and Education
RTU	Regional Training Unit
SCAA	School Curriculum and Assessment Authority
SCCC	Scottish Consultative Council for the Curriculum
SCRE	Scottish Council for Research in Education
SEELB	South Eastern Education and Library Board
SELB	Southern Education and Library Board
SOED	Scottish Office for Education
UNESCO	United Nations Educational, Social and Cultural Organisation
VEC	Values Education Council
VECTOR	Values Education, Consultancy, Training, and Organisational Research
VEEP	Values Education in Europe Project
WELB	Western Education and Library Board
WSI	Whole School Issues

Bibliography

Books, Reports, Papers and Articles

Almond, A.(1990) 'Seven Moral Myths' in *Philosophy* Vol. 65, pp.129-136.

Almond, B. and Compton, A. (eds.) (1989) *Education in a Plural Society*, Social Values Research Centre: University of Hull.

Armstrong, P. (1994) 'Valuing Change and Changing Values', *SCRUTEA Conference Papers*, London.

Barker, D., Halman, L. and Vloet, A. (1992) *The European Values Study 1981-1990* Summary Report, The European Values Group, London: The Gordon Cook Foundation.

Barr, I. (ed.) (1994) *A Sense of belonging - Guidelines for the Humanistic and International Dimension of Education*, Dundee: SCCC.

Barr, I. (1995) 'The Importance of the Preposition', A paper given at the Gordon Cook Foundation Conference, Stirling 1995.

Beck, C. (1990) *Better Schools*, Lewes: The Falmer Press.

Bell, G.H. (1995) Citizenship Values and the European Dimension in Education *Values Education* (ed. Cross, M.) Lancaster: St. Martin's College.

Beresford, B. (1995) Spiritual Development and Inspection *Values Education* (ed. Cross, M.) Vol. 3, No.1, pp.8-11, Lancaster: St. Martins's College.

Berkowitz, M.W. (1995) *The Education of the Complete Moral Person*, Dundee: Northern College.

Bottery, M. (1990) *The Morality of the School: The Theory and Practice of Values in Education*, London: Cassell Publishing.

Bourne, R. (1994) *Commonwealth Values in Education* Human Rights Unit Occasional Paper, London: Commonwealth Secretariat Pall Mall.

Brabeck, M. and Misgeld, D. (1994) Human Rights Education: an issue for moral education *Journal of Moral Education,* Vol.23, No.3 Abingdon: Carfax Publishing Company.

Brady, L. (1990) 'Feeling and Valuing: Educational Imperatives' *Hygie* Vol. IX, No.2 pp. 145-156.

Breen, D. (1995) 'Justice and the Catholic School', *Ethos and Education: The Issue of Justice,* Issue No. 2, Summer, pp.1-11.

British Humanist Association (1994) *Moral Values in Education: A Statement,* London: British Humanist Association.

Carey, P. (1993) 'Dealing with Pupils' Life Crises: 'A Model for Action' *Pastoral Care,* NAPCE, Oxford: Blackwell Publishers, p.12-18.

Carr, D. (1991) *Educating the Virtues,* London Routledge Publishing.

Carr, D. (1991) 'Education and Values', *British Journal of Educational Studies,* Vol. 39, No. 3, p.244-259.

Carr, D. (1992) 'Practical Enquiry, Values and the problem of Educational Theory', *Oxford Review of Education,* Vol.18, No.3, Oxford.

Carr, D. (1992) 'Moral and Religious Education 5-14', *Scottish Educational Review,* Vol. 24, No. 2, pp.111-117.

Carr, D. (1993) 'Moral Values and the Teacher: beyond the paternal and the permissive', *Journal of Philosophy of Education,* Vol. 27, No.2, pp.193-207.

Carr, D. (1993) 'Problems of Values Education', *Values and Values Education,* Centre for Philosophy and Public Affairs, University of St. Andrew's.

Carr, D. (1993) 'Varieties of Goodness in the School Curriculum', *Educational Philosophy and Theory,* Vol. 25 pp.1-17.

Carr, D. (1994) 'Knowledge and Truth in Religious Education', *Journal of Philosophy of Education*, Vol. 28, No.2, pp.221-237.

Carr, D. and Haldane, J. (1993) 'Values and Values Education', *The Victor Cook Memorial Lectures*, St. Andrew's, Centre for Philosophy and Public Affairs, University of St. Andrew's.

Chapman, R. (1995) 'A moral lead from the goldfish bowl', *Times Edueational Supplement* October, 27, p.5.

Cohen, B. (1981) *Education and the Individual*, London: George Allen and Unwin Publishers Ltd.

Compton, A, (1990), *Religious and Values Education in a Plural Society - A Guide for Teachers*, Social Values Research Centre, University of Hull.

Conway, R. (1994) 'Values in Technology Education' in *International Journal of Technology and Design Education* 4, pp.109-116.

Coryton, D. (1995) 'Parents, not politicians, must rule' *Guardian Education*, May 9, p.14.

Cotgrove, S. (1981) 'Risk, Value, conflict and Political Legitimacy', in Griffiths, R.F. *Dealing with Risk*, Manchester University Press, pp.124-125.

Council for Catholic Maintained Schools (CCMS) (1989) *The Catholic Teacher in the Catholic School*. Conference Report, Belfast: Shanway Press.

Council for Catholic Maintained Schools (CCMS) (1990) *From Policy to Planning for Development*, Holywood: CCMS.

Council for Catholic Maintained Schools (CCMS) (1991) *Towards A Whole School Curriculum Policy for Catholic Schools*, Holywood: CCMS.

Council For Catholic Maintained Schools (CCMS) (1995) *Education for Mutual Understanding - A Vision*, Holywood, CCMS.

Cox, E. (1988) 'Explicit and Implicit Moral Education' in *Journal of Moral Education*, Vol. 17, No. 2, pp.92-97.

Cox, E. (1987) 'The Relationship between Beliefs and Values' in *Religious Education*, Vol. 82, No.1, pp.5-19.

Cullingford, C. (ed.) (1985) *Parents, Teachers and Schools*, London: Robert Royce.

Cullingford, C. (1989) *The Primary Teacher:the role of the educator and the purpose*, London: Cassell.

Darlington, L. (1995) 'Glad to meet the family' *Times Educational Supplement*, October 27, p.8.

Davies, L. (1994) 'Focussing on Equal Rights in Teacher Education' *Educational Review*, Vol. 46, No.2, pp.109-121.

Davies, P. (1992) 'The Management of Cross-curricular Themes:A Role for Departments?' *Economic Awareness*, London: SCAA.

Day, C. (1995) 'Rebuild the Fabric of Society', *Times Educational Supplement* March 3, p.9.

Dearing, R. (1994) *The National Curriculum and its Assessment* Final Report, London: School Curriculum and Assessment Authority.

Deen, N. (1995) 'Schools make people grow: Notes on the Supportive School' *Pastoral Care*, NAPCE Oxford:Blackwell Publishers, p.19-25.

Delargey, Fr. P. (1995) 'A Christian Philosophy of Education within the Modern World' in *Ethos and Education: The Issue of Justice*, Issue No. 2, Summer, pp.74-77.

Department of Education for Northern Ireland (DENI) (1990) *Education for Mutual Understanding: A Collection of Papers*, Bangor, Co. Down: Department of Education for Northern Ireland Inspectorate.

Department of Education for Northern Ireland (DENI) (1994) *A Strategic Analysis*, Rathgael, Bangor: DENI.

148

Department of Education for Northern Ireland (DENI) (1995) *Strategic Plan*, Rathgael, Bangor: DENI.

Donaldson, A. (1995) 'Education and Fairness: Myth and Reality' in *Ethos and Education: The Issue of Justice*, Issue No. 2, Summer, p.12-37.

Eisner, E.W. (1994) 'Ethos and Education' in *Perspectives 1*, Scottish Consultative Council on the Curriculum occasional papers, Dundee: SCCC.

Gallagher, A.M. (1995) 'Equality, Contact and Pluralism: Attitudes to Community Relations' *Social Attitudes in Northern Ireland*, Blackstaff Press: Belfast, pp.13-32.

Gardiner, J. (1995) 'Females do better on reflection' *Times Educational Supplement*, October 20, p.9.

Graham, D.C. (1992) *Values Education in England, Wales and Northern Ireland* - A report to the trustees of the Gordon Cook Foundation, Aberdeen.

Gray, J. (1993) *Value-Added Approaches in School Evaluation: The Experiences of three LEAs in England*, Edinburgh: Audit Unit, Her Majesty's Inspectors of Schools, The Scottish Office.

Haigh, G. (1995) 'To be Handled with Care' *Times Educational Supplement* February 10, pp.3-4.

Haldane, J. (1989) 'Metaphysics in the Philosophy of Education', *Journal of Philosophy of Education*, Vol.29.

Haldane, J. (1993) 'The Nature of Values' *Values and Values Education*, Centre for Philosophy and Public Affairs, University of St. Andrew's.

Haldane, J. (ed.) (1994) 'Education, Values and the State', *The Victor Cook Memorial Lectures*, St. Andrew's, Centre for Philosophy and Public Affairs, University of St. Andrew's.

Halstead, J.M. and Taylor, M.J. (eds.) (1996) *Values in Education and Education in Values*, London: Falmer Press.

Hamill, A. (1995) 'Setting the Value-related Areas of EMU and Cultural Heritage in the context of the Northern Ireland Curriculum' in *Values in Education in Northern Ireland Seminar Report* (1996), Montgomery and Smith (eds.).

Hammond, D. and Kirkland, J-P. (1993) 'The Pastoral School at Primary Phase: A Developmental Model' *Pastoral Care*, NAPCE, Oxford:Blackwell Publishers, pp. 3-9.

Harland, J. et al (1996) *The Pilot Phase of the Northern Ireland Curriculum Cohort Study* Report to the Northern Ireland Council for Curriculum, Examinations and Assessment.

Haydon, G. (1993) *Education and the Crisis in Values: Should we be Philosophical about it?* The London File Papers for the Institute of Education, London: Tufnell Press.

Higham, A. (1994) 'Tomorrow's School' in *20/20 Vision Series SHA.*, Banbury.

Hurt, J. (1990) 'Parental Involvement in Schools: A historical perspective' in *Parents, Teachers and Schools,* Cullingford (ed.), London: Robert Boyce.

Jackson, M. (1995) 'Pathways through the moral maze' *Times Educational Supplement* February 2, p.6.

Jarrett, J.L. (1991) *The Teaching of Values: Caring and Appreciation,* Routledge: London.

John, P.D. and Osborn, A. (1992) 'The influence of school ethos on pupils' citizenship attitudes', *Educational Review,* Vol. 44, No. 2.

Joyce, S. (1992) *Values Education in Bishopbriggs School,* Aberdeen: The Gordon Cook Foundation.

Joyce, S. (1995) 'The role of Spiritual Values' *Values Education* (ed. Cross, M.) Vol. 3, No. 1, pp.19-26. Lancaster: S. Martin's College.

Klein, R. (1995) 'Lost in Wonder', *Times Educational Supplement,* April 28.

Klein, R. (1995) 'Devilish Dilemmas', *Times Ednal Supplement*, June 16, p.5.

Kohlberg, L. (1978) 'Stages of Moral Development', *Stage Theories of Cognitive and Moral Development: Criticisms and Applications*, Cambridge, Mass., Harvard University Review, pp. 23-92.

Laar, B. (1995) 'Way out of the moral muddle' *Times Educational Supplement*, April 28, p.4.

Lee, (1995) 'Play the Game', *Times Educational Supplement*, October 27 1995, p.17.

Leicester, M. (1989) *Multicultural Education: From Theory to Practice*, Windsor: NFER Nelson.

Leicester, M. (1992) 'Values, Cultural Conflict and Education' in M. Leicester and M.J. Taylor (eds.) *Ethics, Ethnicity and Education*, London: Kogan Page.

Leicester, M. and Taylor, M.J. (eds.) (1992) *Ethics, Ethnicity and Education*, London: Kogan Page.

Lynch, F. (1995) 'The Idea of a Catholic School' in *Ethos and Education: The Issue of Justice*, Issue No. 2, Summer, p.67-73.

Martin, P. (1994) 'Values in Management - Education and Development', Bristol Business School, University of West of England, Bristol.

Meighan, R. (1981) *A Sociology of Learning*, Eastbourne: Holt, Reinhart and Winston.

McAdam, N. (1993) 'Cross Purposes', *Times Ednl Supplement,* April 15, p.7.

McGettrick, B.J. (1992) 'Some Implications for Education', *The European Values Study Summary Report*, The European Values Group, London: The Gordon Cook Foundation, pp.52-56.

McGettrick, B.J. (1995) 'Values and Educating the Whole Person' in *Perspectives 2*, Scottish Consultative Council on the Curriculum occasional papers, Dundee: SCCC.

McLaughlin, T.H. (1995) 'Public Values, Private Values and Educational Responsibility' in *Values, Education and Responsibility,* Centre for Philosophy and Public Affairs, University of St. Andrew's.

McPhail, P. (1972) *Moral Education in the Secondary School.* London: Longmann.

Montgomery, A. and Smith, A. (1996) *Values in Education in Northern Ireland: A Seminar Report.*

Moon, P. (1993) *Humanities and Arts Education: A review of issues prepared as part of the OECD/CERI project, 'The Curriculum Redefined'.*

Northern Ireland Curriculum Council (NICC) (1993) *An Exercise in the Dimensions of the Curriculum,* An Internal report (unpublished), Stranmillis, Belfast: NICC.

Northern Ireland Council for Educational Development (NICED) (1989) *Education for Mutual Understanding: A Planning Guide for Teachers,* Belfast: NICED.

O'Grady, C. (1995) 'Someone to turn to' *Times Educational Supplement,* October 27, p.5.

Office for Standards in Education (OFSTED) (1993 revised). *Framework for Inspection,* London: HMSO.

Office for Standards in Education (OFSTED) (1993) (revised May 1994) *Handbook of the Inspection of Schools,* London: HMSO.

Office for Standards in Education (OFSTED) (1994) *Spiritual, Moral, Social and Cultural Development ,* An OFSTED Discussion Paper, Office for Standards in Education, London: HMSO.

Osborne, R.D. (1995) 'Social Attitudes in Northern Ireland: Education', *Social Attitudes in Northern Ireland ,* Belfast: Blackstaff Press, pp.33-48.

Pickard, W. (1995) 'To point down the road to ethics', *Times Educational Supplement* June 9, p.23.

Pring, R. (1992) 'Education for a Pluralist Society' in M. Leicester and M.J. Taylor (eds.) *Ethics, Ethnicity and Education,* London: Kogan Page.

Pring, R. (1994) 'Liberal and Vocational Education: A conflict of Value' in *Education, Values and the State,* Centre for Philosophy and Public Affairs, University of St. Andrew's.

Pybus, E. (1995) 'Values, Education and Responsibility', in *Values, Education and Responsibility,* Centre for Philosophy and Public Affairs, University of St. Andrew's.

Pyke, N. (1995) 'RE slowly starts to rise from the dead', *Time Educational Supplement* October 13, p.15.

Pyke, N. 'Inspectors edge into moral maze' *Times Educational Supplement* March 4, p.7.

Reynolds, D. (1995) 'Some very peculiar practice' *Times Educational Supplement* June 16, p.19.

Richardson, N. (1990) *Religious Education as if EMU really mattered,* Lisburn, Northern Ireland: Christian Education Movement.

Richardson, N. (1992) 'Roots, If not Wings!, Where did EMU come from?', Keynote Paper at Conference, *EMU in Transition,* Newcastle, Co. Down.

Richardson, N. and Bell, A. (1995) *Who's Who in EMU and Cultural Heritage 1995-1996* Belfast, The FOCUS Group.

Robb, W.M. (ed.) (1991) *Values Education: Some Recent Developments in Scotland,* Aberdeen: The Gordon Cook Foundation.

Robb, W.M. (ed.) (1991) *Values Education: Some Ways Forward,* Aberdeen: The Gordon Cook Foundation.

Rodger, A. (1989) *Think Again About Values in Education,* Aberdeen: Northern College of Education.

Rodger, A. (1992) *Towards a Position on Moral Education in Schools,* Aberdeen: Northern College of Education.

Rodger, A. (1993) *Moral Education: A Distance Learning Module for Secondary Teachers,* Aberdeen: Northern College of Education.

Rodger, A. (ed.) (1995) *Values Education: A view from Scotland - Proceedings from the Gordon Cook Foundation Conference, Stirling 1995,* Aberdeen: The Gordon Cook Foundation.

Rodger, I.A. and Richardson, J.A.S. (1985) *Self-Evaluation for Primary Schools,* London: Hodder and Stoughton.

Rowe, D. (1992) 'Law-related Education: An Overview' *Cultural Diversity and the Schools* Vol. 4, Human rights, Education and Global Responsibilities, London: The Falmer Press.

Rowe, D. (1992) 'The Citizen as a Moral Agent - the Development of a Continuous and Progressive Conflict-based Citizenship Curriculum' *Curriculum* Vol.13, No. 3, pp.178-187.

Rowe, D. (1992) 'The Citizen and Law - Teaching about the Rights and Duties of Citizenship' *Education for Citizenhsip - Ideas and Perspectives for Cross-curricular Study* (eds. Baglin Jones, E. and Jones, N.). London: Kogan Page.

Rowe, D. (1995) *Developing Spiritual, Moral and Social Values through a Citizenship Programme for Primary Schools,* London: The Citizenship Foundation.

Rowe, D. (1995) 'Education for Citizenship in Europe' *Educating European Citizens: Citizenship and the European Dimension* (ed. Bell. G.), London: David Fulton Publishers, pp.46-56.

Rowe, D. (1995) *Transmitting Citizenship Values: a European Perspective,* London: The Citizenship Foundation.

Rutter, M., Maughan, B., Mortimore, P. and Ouston, J. (1979) *Fifteen Thousand Hours: Secondary Schools and their effects on Children,* London: Open Books Publishing Ltd.

School Curriculum and Assessment Authority (SCAA) (1995) *Spiritual and Moral Development* SCAA Discussion Papers No.3, London: SCAA.

Scottish Consultative Council on the Curriculum (SCCC) (1986) *More than feelings of Concern: Guidance and Scottish Secondary Schools* The Report of the Scottish Central Committee on Guidance, Dundee: SCCC.

Scottish Consultative Council on the Curriculum (SCCC) (1991) *Values in Education,* Dundee: SCCC.

Scottish Consultative Council on the Curriculum (SCCC) (1994) *Personal and Social Education*, Conference Report, Dundee: SCCC.

Scottish Consultative Council on the Curriculum (SCCC) (1994) *School Climate and Ethos*, Conference Report, Dundee: SCCC.

Scottish Consultative Council on the Curriculum (SCCC) (1995) *A Sense of Belonging (Reflections on Curricular issues; 4),* Dundee: SCCC.

Scottish Consultative Council on the Curriculum (SCCC) (1995) *The Heart of the Matter: A Paper for Discussion and Development,* Dundee: SCCC.

Scottish Council for Research in Education (SCRE) (1994) *66th Annual Report 1993-94,* Edinburgh: SCRE.

Scottish Office Audit Unit (The) (1993) *Standards and Quality in Scottish Schools 1991-92,* A report by Her Majesty's Inspectors of Schools, Edinburgh: The Scottish Office Education Department.

Scottish Office Audit Unit, (The), (1993), *The Role Of Development Plans in Managing School Effectiveness - Headteachers' Views,* A report commissioned for Her Majesty's Inspectorate of Schools, Edinburgh: The Scottish Office.

Sedgwick, F. (1994) *Personal, Social and Moral Education,* London:David Fulton Publishers.

Sedgwick, F. (1995) 'Dealing with Bullying' *Primary File* 24, pp.115-118, London:Primary File publishing.

Singh, B. (1995) 'Shared values, Particular values and Education for a Multi-Cultural Society', *Educational Review* Vol. 47, No.1 p.116 -127.

Smith, A. (1993) 'Shared Governance: Maintained Participation in Integrated Education' in *Education for a Change: Integrated Education and Community Relations in Northern Ireland* (ed. Moffat, C), Belfast Fortnight Educational Trust, pp.132-152.

Smith, A. (1994) 'Education for Mutual Understanding', *CRC News*, Belfast, Northern Ireland Community Relations Council.

Smith, A. (1994) *The EMU Promoting School* - Report of a conference on Education for Mutual Understanding and Cultural Heritage, Coleraine, Northern Ireland: Centre for the Study of Conflict, University of Ulster.

Smith, A. and Dunn, S. (1990) *Extending Inter School Links: An Evaluation of Contact between Protestant and Catholic Pupils in Northern Ireland*, Coleraine, Northern Ireland: Centre for the Study of Conflict, University of Ulster.

Smith, A. and Robinson, A. (1992) *Education for Mutual Understanding: Perceptions and Policy*, Coleraine: Centre for the Study of Conflict, University of Ulster.

Smith, A. and Robinson, A. (1996) *Education for Mutual Understanding: The Initial Statutory Years*, Coleraine: Centre for the Study of Conflict, University of Ulster.

Tate, N. (1995) 'Friends, subjects and citizens' *Times Educational Supplement*, June 11, p.14.

Taylor, M. J. (1992) *Citizenship Education in the UK: An Overview*, Slough: National Foundation for Educational Research.

Taylor, M. (ed.) (1994) *Values in Education: A Directory of Research and Resources*, Slough: National Foundation for Educational Research.

Taylor, M. (ed.) (1994) *Values Education in Europe: A Comparative overview of a survey of 26 countries in 1993*, Slough: NFER/CIDREE/UNESCO.

Thomas, L. (1995) 'Beware the Staffroom minefield' *Times Educational Supplement*, October 27, p.12.

Thorpe, T. (1995) *Young Citizen's Passport: Your Guide to the Law,* The Citizenship Foundation, London: Hodder and Stoughton.

Tomlinson, P. and Quinton, M. (eds.) (1986) *Values Across the Curriculum,* London: The Falmer Press.

Troyna, B. and Hatcher, R. (1991) 'British Schools for British Citizens?' *Oxford Review of Education,* Vol.17, No.3, pp.287-299.

Turner, R. (1991) 'The Presentation and Display of Children's Work' *Pastoral Care,* NAPCE, Oxford: Blackwell Publishers.

Tyrrell, J. (1995) *The Quaker Peace Education Project 1988-1994: Developing Untried Strategies,* Coleraine: The Centre for the Study of Conflict, University of Ulster.

Ulanowsky, C, (1991) *Education for Personal Relationships - Guidelines for Teachers,* Social Values Research Centre: University of Hull.

Ulster Bank (1994) *The Enterprising School,* Belfast: Ulster Bank Ltd.

Vatican Council (1966) *Gravissimum Educationis,* paper given at CCMS Conference entitled 'The Catholic School at the Service of Society', (Daly, Bishop C.), Belfast: Shanway Press.

Walker J. (1992) *Violence and Conflict Resolution in Schools - A study of the teaching of inter-personal problem-solving skills in primary and secondary schools in Europe,* Strasbourg: Council of Europe, Council for Cultural Co-operation.

Warnock, Baroness (1994) 'Educational Obligations of the State' in *Education, Values and the State,* The Victor Cook Memorial lectures, Centre for Philosophy and Public Affairs, University of St. Andrew's.

Western Education and Library Board (1995) *The Strabane Initiative: Project Funding Application,* WELB.

Whitty G., Rowe, G. and Aggleton P. (1994) 'Subjects and Themes in the Secondary School Curriculum' in *Research Papers in Education,* Vol.9, No.2, June 1994.

Williams, E.A. (1993) 'The Contribution of Physical Education to Personal and Social Development' *Pastoral Care* NAPCE, Oxford:Blackwell Publishers, pp.21-25.

Wilson, D. and Dunn, S. (1989) *Integrated Schools: Information for Parents,* Coleraine: Centre for the Study of Conflict, University of Ulster.

Wilson, J. (1977) *Philosophy and Practical Education,* London: Routledge & Kegan Paul.

Wilson, J. (1979) *Preface to the Philosophy of Education,* London: Routledge & Kegan Paul.

Wilson, J. (1986) *What Philosophy can do,* London: Macmillan.

Wilson, J. (1987) *A Preface to Morality,* London: Macmillan.

Wilson, J. (1990) *A New Introduction to Moral Education,* London: Cassell Educational Limited.

Wilson, K. (1995) 'Beyond Comparison', *Times Educational Supplement,* February 2, p.15.

Wilson, P.S. (1975) 'The Use of Value Terms in Discussions of Education', *Journal of Value Inquiry,* Vol. 9, No.3, pp.186-200.

Winkley, D. (1985) 'The School's view of Parents', *Parents, Teachers and Schools,* Cullingford (ed.), London: Robert Royce.

Wise, C. (1994) The Flexible Use of Values Criteria,*Values Education* (ed. Cross, M.) Vol.2, No.2, pp.19-22. Lancaster: S. Martin's College.

Woodhead, C. (1995) Any partners for inspection tango? *Times Educational Supplement* October 27, p.6.

Curriculum and Staff Development Materials

Conroy, J. (1995) *Values Education: Making a Start* (video), St. Andrew's College, Glasgow, The Gordon Cook Foundation.

Cross, M. (1995) *Values Education: A Staff Development Manual for Secondary schools*, Lancaster: Framework Press.

Council for Education in World Citizenship (CEWC) (1991/2) *Broadsheet* London: CEWC.

Department of Education for Northern Ireland (DENI) (1993) *Core Syllabus for Religious Studies*, DENI/HMSO.

Joyce, S. (1994) *Values Education Resource book: Ideas for promoting children's moral development,* Aylesbury: Ginn and Co, Ltd. in association with the Gordon Cook Foundation.

Mills, S. (1995) *Managing People through Change: A Guide for Schools and Colleges*, Lancaster:Framework Press.

National Curriculum Council (NCC) (1989) *The National Curriculum and Whole Curriculum Planning: Preliminary Guidance,* Circular No. 6, York: NCC.

National Curriculum Council (NCC) (1990) *The Whole Curriculum*, Curriculum Guidance 3, York: NCC.

National Curriculum Council (NCC) (1990) *Education for Economic and Industrial Understanding,* Curriculum Guidance 4, York: NCC.

National Curriculum Council (NCC) (1990) *Education for Citizenship*, Curriculum Guidance 8, York: NCC.

Northern College (1994) *All Things Considered* (video), Values Education Project, Dundee.

Northern Ireland Curriculum Council (NICC) (1989) Cross-curricular Themes, Stranmillis College, Belfast: NICC.

Northern Ireland Curriculum Council (NICC) (1992) *Economic Awareness - A Cross-curricular theme,* Stranmillis College, Belfast: NICC.

Northern Ireland Curriculum Council (NICC) (1992) *Information Technology - A Cross-curricular theme,* Stranmillis College, Belfast: NICC.

Northern Ireland Curriculum Council (NICC) (1992) *Careers Education - A Cross-Curricular theme,* Stranmillis College, Belfast: NICC.

Northern Ireland Curriculum Council (NICC) (1992) *Education for Mutual Understanding- A cross-curricular theme,* Stranmillis College, Belfast: NICC.

Northern Ireland Curriculum Council (NICC) (1992) *Cultural Heritage - A Cross-curricular theme,* Stranmillis College, Belfast: NICC.

Northern Ireland Curriculum Council (NICC) (1992) *Health Education - A Cross-curricular theme,* Stranmillis College, Belfast: NICC.

Northern Ireland Curriculum Council (NICC) (1992) *Thinking European - Ideas for Integrating a European Dimension into the Curriculum,* Stranmillis, Belfast: NICC.

Northern Ireland Curriculum Council (NICC) (1993) *Equal Opportunities in the N.I. Curriculum: Gender Equality (Post Primary)* Stranmillis College, Belfast: NICC.

Nuffield Design and Technology (1995) *Student's Book,* Essex: Longman Group Ltd.

Nuffield Design and Technology (1995) *Study Guide,* Essex: Longman Group Ltd.

OFSTED (1994) *Spiritual, Moral, Social and Cultural Development,* Discussion Paper, London: OFSTED

Rodger, A. and Squires, J. (eds.) (1995) Values Education Project, *A handbook for School Values Development,* Dundee: Northern College.

Rodger, A. and Squires, J. (eds.) (1996) *Explorations in School Values,* Dundee: Northern College.

Rowe, D. and Newton, J. (1994) *You, Me, Us - Social and Moral Responsibility for Primary Schools,* London: The Citizenship Foundation/The Home Office.

Schools Curriculum and Assessment Authority (SCAA) (1995) *Spiritual and Moral Development,* Discussion Paper No. 3, London: SCAA.

Schools Curriculum and Assessment Authority (SCAA) (1996) *Education for Adult Life: The Spiritual and Moral Development of Young People,* Discussion Paper No. 6, London: SCAA.

Schools Curriculum and Assessment Authority (SCAA) (1996) *Consultation on Values in Education and the Community,* COM/96/CO8, London: SCAA.

Scottish Consultative Council on the Curriculum (SCCC) (1993) *Working Together: A Pack for Parents and Teachers* Dundee: SCCC.

Scottish Consultative Council on the Curriculum (1995) *Personal and Social Development 5-15 exemplification: The Whole School Approach - A Staff Development Workshop,* Dundee: SCCC.

Scottish Consultative Council on the Curriculum (1996) *Climate for Learning: The Learning School, a resource pack,* Dundee: SCCC.

Scottish Office Education Department (SOED) (1992) Curriculum and Assessment in Scotland National Guidelines, *Religious and Moral Education 5-14* , Edinburgh: SOED.

Scottish Office Education Department (SOED) (1992) Using Ethos Indicators in Primary School Self-Evaluation - Taking Account of the Views of Pupils, Parents and Teachers, Edinburgh: HMI Scotland SOED.

Scottish Office Education Department (SOED) (1992) Using Ethos Indicators in Secondary School Self -Evaluation - Taking Account of the Views of Pupils, Parents and Teachers, Edinburgh: HMI Scotland, SOED.

Smith, R. (1995) *Managing Pupil Behaviour: In-house Training Materials for Teachers,* Lancaster: Framework Press.

Speak Your Piece (1996) *Exploring Controversial Issues in Northern Ireland,* guidance booklet which accompanies a video of five Channel 4 television programmes, Coleraine, School of Education, University of Ulster.

Index

development -
    affective, 70,
    cognitive, 43, 51, 118
    cultural, 18, 21, 27, 33, 35, 88
    emotional, 35, 70, 88, 89, 117, 118
    intellectual, 27, 35, 59, 88
    inter-personal, 88
    mental, 47, 88
    moral, 4, 16, 18, 20, 21, 25, 27, 33, 35, 70, 88, 89, 116, 118
    personal, 19, 25, 26, 33, 59, 70, 73, 75, 79, 88, 90, 117, 118, 121, 122
    professional, 23, 25, 84, 117, 120, 121, 122
    physical, 27, 33, 35, 44, 47, 52, 73, 88
    school, 19, 20
    social, 16, 18, 19, 20, 25, 35, 49, 59, 70, 73, 88, 89, 90, 111, 117, 118
    spiritual, 4, 16, 18, 21, 22, 27, 33, 35, 55, 88,101, 116
    staff, 24, 99, 120
    whole child, 10, 33, 71, 89, 93, 94
developmental dimensions, 2
discipline - see Curriculum Informal
Drama - see Curriculum, Formal
drama therapy, 56, 113

Economic Awareness - see Cross-curricular themes
Education and Library Boards (ELBs), 8, 28, 30, 37
    Western Education and Library Board, 29, 31
    North-Eastern Education and Library Board, 29
Education for Mutual Understanding (EMU) - see Cross-curricular themes
    EMU Promoting School, 29
emotional issues, 48, 55, 56, 66
English - see Curriculum, Formal
Environment and Society - see Curriculum, Formal
environment, 21, 32, 44, 58, 59, 61, 64, 87, 112
    projects, 87, 96
ethics, 20, 24, 25, 88
ethos, see Curriculum, Hidden
Ethos and Performance Indicators, 11, 12, 19, 20
European Values Group, 14-15
European Values Study, 14-15

evaluation - see school evaluation
examinations, 40, 46, 64, 65, 68, 83, 105, 109
Extra-curricular activities - see Curriculum, Informal

Formal Curriculum- see Curriculum, Formal
Forum on Community Understanding on Schools (FOCUS), 29
French - see Curriculum, Formal

GCSE - see examinations
gender issues, 10, 42, 46, 54, 62
Geography - see Curriculum, Formal
German - see Curriculum, Formal
Gordon Cook Foundation, 22, 115
grammar schools - see schools, grammar

Hamill, Aidan, 27
Haldane, John, 3, 24
Harland, John et al, 7, 39, 57, 72-73, 81, 101, 106-107
Health Education - see Cross-curricular themes
headteachers, 8, 86, 88, 92, 96, 100, 103, 108, 109
Hidden Curriculum - see Curriculum, Hidden
History - see Curriculum, Formal
Home Economics - see Curriculum, Formal
homework, 94
human rights, 14, 15, 20, 32, 62, 79

identity, 10, 30, 54, 60, 65, 70, 76, 81, 88
integrated schools - see schools, integrated
Informal Curriculum - see Curriculum, Informal
Information Technology (IT) - see Cross-curricular themes
inspection, 18, 77, 85
Irish - see Curriculum, Formal

Raising School Standards Initiative, 30
relationships - see Curriculum, Hidden
Religious Education (RE) - see Curriculum, Formal
Research into Moral, Spiritual and Cultural Understanding and Education,
(RIMSCUE), 21, 25
Rowe, Don, 20

Science - see Curriculum, Formal
Science and Technology - see Curriculum, Formal
Scottish Consultative Council for the Curriculum (SCCC), 2, 4, 11, **19**, 99, 115
Scottish Office for Education (HMI), 11, **19-20**
school -
    culture, 100, 109-110
    evaluation, **11-12**, 18, 19-20, 124
    timetable, 10, 48, 57, 65, 71, 99, 101, 120
schools -
    controlled, 9, 10, 11, 68, 82, 86, 88, 109-110
    grammar, 9, 10. 46, 51, 57, 71, 72, 82, 83, 86, 102, 103, 109-110
    integrated, 9, 10, 69, 82, 93, 107
    maintained, 9, 10, 30, 68, 82, 86, 93, 100, 109-110, 112-113
    primary, 9, 10, 11, 12, 19, 20, 22, 25, 31, 37, 69, 82, 95, 103, 107, 110,
        113
    post-primary, 9, 10, 19, 20, 22, 31, 87, 88, 95, 97, 103, 107, 110
    secondary, 9, 10, 11, 43, 46, 51, 57, 71, 72, 82, 83, 86, 91, 103, 107, 109
    special, 9, 10, 52, 82, 87, 93, 94, 95, 106, 107, 113
School's Curriculum and Assessment Authority (SCAA), 4, 11, 16, 65, 116
secondary schools - see schools, secondary
sex education, 44, 65
Speak your Piece project, 30
social dimension, 2, 24, 51
special needs, 10, 50, 52, 56, 77
special school - see schools, special
sports, 35, 53, 55, 86
spiritual dimension, 55-56
staffroom- see Curriculum, Informal
Streaming - see Curriculum, Hidden

Taylor, Monica, 2, 3, 13, 15
Teacher role, 9, 10, 78, 90, 121 (also see Curriculum, Hidden)
    trainers, 8, 13, 122
    training, 8, 13, 22, 25, 43, 53, 79, 84, 121, 122
        inservice, 23, 45, 58, 79, 84, 121, 122
Technology - see Curriculum, Formal
Tomlinson, P and Quinton, M., 3, 40
Transfer Procedure - see Hidden Curriculum

values -
    aesthetic, 23, 51
    Christian, 14, 64, 66, 93, 100, 120
    corporate, 61
    cultural, 37, 39, 41, 42, 45, 47, 49, 51, 54, 58, 64, 70
    dimension, 1, 10, 27, 37, 78-79, 83-84, 115, 118, 119, 122
    economic, 23
    emotional, 37, 38, 44, 47, 51, 54, 58, 64
    environmental, 23
    intellectual, 37, 38, 40, 41, 42, 58, 71
    moral, 4, 23, 26, 37, 39, 41, 43, 44, 45, 47, 50, 58, 64, 89
    personal, 10, 16, 25, 48, 61
    physical, 37, 38, 44, 47, 51, 58, 59, 64
    political, 41, 54
    social, 23, 37, 38, 41, 42, 44, 45, 47, 51, 54, 58, 62, 64
    spiritual, 37, 51, 64
    technological, 23
Values and Visions Project, 22-23
values education, 2, 3, 12, 13, 14, 17, 20, 21, 22, 24, 26, 33, 66, 83, 115, 119
Values Education, Consultancy, Training and Organisational Research
    (VECTOR), 22, 25
Values Education Council, 21, 115
Values Education Project, 24
Values in European Education Project (VEEP), 13-14

"whole school", 2, 3, 24, 93
    approach, 19, 23, **30-31**, 32, 33
    initiatives, 13, 29, 93
    policy, 18, 30, 93
Wilson, John, 3, 24, 40